LOOKING BACK

LOOKING BACK

LOOKING BACK

two autobiographical essays

DOUGLAS HARDING

The Shollond Trust
London

Published by The Shollond Trust
87B Cazenove Road, London N16 6BB, England
www.headless.org
headexchange@gn.apc.org

The Shollond Trust is a UK charitable trust, reg. no. 1059551

ISBN 978-1-914316-47-0

Cover photograph: Sam Blight
Cover design: rangsgraphics.com
Interior design: Richard Lang

PREFACE

Douglas Harding's great book *The Hierarchy of Heaven and Earth* — a game-changer in terms of how we understand our place in the universe — was published in 1952, when Harding was 43. (The original huge version is now also available. Highly recommended.) In this opus magnum Harding takes the reader with him on a journey through all the physical and mental layers of himself, from the Whole at his periphery down through his suprahuman, human, and infrahuman layers, to the *nothingness* at his Centre. Then, having mapped out this mandala-like structure in *space* and indicated how he, the universe-embracing system that he is, functions (vertically), Harding introduces the *time* dimension. Since it is *his* past and *his* future he is looking into — from his timeless Centre — the chapters on time are therefore *autobiographical*. However, this mind- and body-expanding (and contracting) trip through whatever or whoever Douglas Harding 'really' is, reveals hardly anything about Douglas Harding's *personal* life — which of course is appropriate given the nature of the work.

From time to time Harding *did* write about himself *personally*, the first time being before *The Hierarchy of Heaven and Earth*. In the mid-1930s, when he was in his mid-twenties, Harding wrote more than a dozen short stories, many of which are thinly-veiled accounts of his childhood. Harding wrote these 'tales' (gathered together under the title *The Crimson Tiger*) some five years after making a profoundly significant decision: when he was 21 he left the Plymouth Brethren, the religion he had been brought up in. As a result — as a punishment — his parents cut off from him. In these stories Harding was looking back and reflecting on his young life prior to that break from his family. (This would not be the last time Harding employed fiction as a vehicle for sorting out and presenting to the world the way he saw himself.)

Harding spent his thirties and early forties writing *The Hierarchy of Heaven and Earth*. He once described writing *The Hierarchy* as 'a ten-year mystical experience'. It profoundly changed the way he saw himself. Then, when Harding was about fifty he wrote *On Having No Head*. It was published by the Buddhist Society in 1961 with the idea that an expanded version would soon follow. Though Harding did write several more parts for it, that larger version never appeared. One of the extra parts he wrote was the first essay in this book, *An Autobiographical Essay*. Having discovered so much about himself and the world, Harding decided it was a good moment to look back and reflect on his life. As well as attempting to understand himself better, Harding hoped that some of what he had learned might prove helpful to others. Harding's self-awareness, his ability to see and articulate the trajectory of his life, is impressive.

Since *An Autobiographical Essay* had not been published, Harding stored it away in a drawer. Years later he took it out and, revising it slightly, renamed it *Right About Face: Confessions of an Ex-Plymouth Brother*. It is this version we are publishing here. ('Right about face' is a military command — Harding was a major in the Second World War. It's an order to turn completely around, 180°, so that you end up facing in the opposite direction, which for Harding was a metaphor for turning your attention round 180°, from *what you are looking at* to *what you are looking out of*. 'Right about face' is also a play on words: be right about your face — right about where it is... and where it isn't!)

Harding wrote the second essay, *The Mystical Viewpoint: Autobiography of a Simpleto*n, when he was eighty. Obviously since the first essay a lot of water had flowed under the bridge of his life, so not surprisingly this second essay has a different feel from the first one. Having developed in all kinds of ways over the previous thirty years, Harding was now looking back and reflecting on his life from a new viewpoint. (About the same time as Harding wrote this essay, he also wrote *The Spectre in the Lake*, a fictional story that was also — essentially — autobiographical.)

One of the differences between these two essays is that in the second Harding describes his childhood in greater depth. They say that in old age, long-term memory is sharper than short-term memory. Harding portrays his childhood relationship with his parents in lively detail and with the increased understanding and tolerance, particularly towards his mother, that came with his advanced years. And in the second essay Harding's sense of humour is in much greater evidence. But though the two essays are different, the same motive underlies them both — writing about himself personally was really just an excuse for him to share the experience and meaning of Who we all really are. Harding never stopped trying to give away the Pearl of great price.

Richard Lang

Contents

ESSAY ONE

AUTOBIOGRAPHICAL ESSAY

or

RIGHT ABOUT FACE: CONFESSIONS OF AN EX-PLYMOUTH BROTHER

All writing on spiritual things, if it is alive and real, is surely a special kind of confession, giving first-hand expression to first-hand experience, no matter how carefully the author may take cover behind a screen of decorous impersonality. If his 'way' or 'teaching' arises directly out of the trials and discoveries of his own intimate life, it does at least stand a chance of being really helpful and interesting to others caught up in similar adventures; and nothing much is gained by disguising its source.

In any case it is a healthy exercise to look back from time to time, and to notice — with astonishment — how the past is always changing, always in the making and never done with. One's earlier years only begin to make sense in retrospect; for life, as Kierkegaard observed, is lived forwards but understood backwards. The value and meaning come out in the end, if only one is patient and open-minded enough; and until they do so one is ill at ease, if not actually ill. Present maturity, wholeness, health, mean that one denies or undervalues no part of one's past; in particular, its more disgraceful episodes are fully faced and accepted, and so cease to give trouble.

More than this, it sometimes turns out that the silliest and most shaming aberrations of childhood and youth — those nastinesses which one hopes have been finally lived down if not forgotten — are the very clues needed to explain and complete the present. Looking back, one may at last come to detect at every stage the work of that supremely wise and loving Guiding Hand (call It what you like) which seemed so conspicuously absent at the time.

In this essay I want to pick up some of the seemingly loose threads of my childhood and youth and early manhood, and follow them through, to see how they tie up with the realisations of the present. In other words, the question I am now asking is: what, looking back, appear to have been the really formative factors and influences in my own spiritual life, and what contribution are they making now?

The Brethren

My parents, like my paternal grandparents before them, belonged to the sect of fundamentalist Christians known to the world as the Exclusive Plymouth Brethren — a title they disowned; for themselves they were simply *the* Brethren, the Saints, the Meeting. Their theology wasn't remarkable: they were of the evangelical school that insists on the total depravity of unregenerate human nature, the justification of the sinner by faith alone, and the exclusive authority of the Bible — that is to say, their own naive and arbitrary interpretation of the Bible. It was their zeal, the uncompromising way they put their beliefs into practice, that was remarkable. Utterly convinced they were the Chosen People, the Brethren, keeping their contacts with the outside world to a minimum, had developed a strange ingrown cult, often morbid in its narrowness and enthusiasm, with its own jargon and even its own pronunciation. Within the tiny close circle of Brothers and Sisters and their children, the emphasis was all on a sort of love, love real or worked-up or simulated — love of Jesus, of God, of the "saved" Brethren, in that order, and of nobody else — while outside that quiet enclave raged the hateful, loveless, frightening, wicked, lost world, soon to be punished in Hell fire. Such was the world picture I inherited.

Our family day began and ended with Bible reading (father relentlessly working through the lot from *Genesis* to *Revelation* not excluding the genealogical tables of *Kings* and *Chronicles* and 'extempore' prayers, which always turned out to be virtually the same as yesterday's. No newspapers, no radio, almost no books except the Brethren's own esoteric publications, no "worldly" visitors, no real secular interests at all, were allowed in our home; and of course we had no idea what went on in dance-halls and theatres and cinemas, though the posters supplied our imaginations with hints that confirmed our worst suspicions. School games were discouraged. School prize-givings, because they were known to include theatrical sketches, weren't attended. Novels, and other unnecessary books smuggled into the house, were when discovered liable to solemn burning. On two or three evenings during the week, and three times on the Lord's Day, the Brethren met for prayer, or Bible reading and discussion, or the celebration of the Lord's Supper, or the preaching of the Gospel. Since the gathering was usually small (for some time my father was the only local Brother, and Sisters were forbidden to speak) the meetings were largely exercises in sitting still for seventy-five minutes, with closed or half-closed eyes, silently "meditating".

This was unusual discipline for a healthy and energetic child of four upwards, but before long it became second nature to sit still. No doubt most of the time was spent day-dreaming, but I did learn some of the satisfaction to be had by clearing the mind and just staring at things. For instance, I found that, if I looked fixedly and without thinking at whatever lay ahead — maybe at the red-and-black hassocks or the herringbone pattern of the coconut-matting — I could make it creep up to me, its distance abolished. I suppose I started this game when I was about five, and kept it up because it was more than just fun: it was the exercise of my own private magic, of a secret power. Actually, of course, it was a trick, a case of letting the eyes relax and focus at a distance, and anyone can do it.

It was also more than a trick. It was a temporary unlearning of the learned faculty of "distancing" the outside world — all of which is in reality presented right here and not over there: the scene does in fact coincide with its observer. It was an early preview of a realisation that later on was to become all-important to me — the fact that I am what I see; that not a hair's breadth separates me from my world; that my wealth right here, ranging from those stars to these hands and feet is infinite.

As I grew older, I often tried to concentrate on the kind of things I was supposed to think about in Meetings, such as God's love for me, the past sufferings and present glory of the Lord Jesus, and my own response to his sacrifice — but without much success. I found it very difficult to work up, and impossible to sustain, warm feelings of devotion to an external deity — and though the Brethren often talked about the Kingdom of Heaven within, and Christ in our hearts,

He remained in practice outside. Even when I did feel some real emotion of love or pity or trust, I very soon became very much aware of it; and, inevitably, as soon as it was inspected and encouraged, it disappeared, and I was left in a state of spiritual dryness and vacuity. I didn't know then what I know now, that this conscious emptiness was awareness of my true state and the beginning of true meditation. So there followed discouragement, anxiety, and an intermittent sense of guilt at my heartlessness, my lack of love.

However, at the age of twelve I did manage to struggle through the requisite experience of conversion or salvation, which was for the Brethren the passport into their community. To be reckoned altogether genuine and complete, it had to include a sudden collapse of the everyday self, a breakdown of the ego's resistance to the overtures of divine love, and an unqualified act of faith in the saving efficacy of the sacrifice on the Cross, no matter how wretched or depraved one's human condition might be. In short, it had to be a kind of death, followed by a new life in Christ and out of the world. I need hardly say that my own "salvation" fell far short of this ideal pattern. It owed much to imitation (I felt what I felt I should be feeling) and much also to fear. Hell fire, though frightening enough, was remote. The immediate threat, the ever-present worry, was lest I should be left behind on earth at the time of the Lord's Second Coming: for at any moment my parents, with all the rest of the saved ones, were liable to be caught up to Heaven with the Lord, abandoning me with the rest of the damned to a life of unimaginable despair, followed by the eternal torments of Hell. The immense love of Christ for me on the one hand, and on the other the immense agony I should certainly suffer if I didn't quickly

give in to that love, lent a double urgency to every Gospel
Meeting. "Behold, now is the accepted time; behold, now is
the day of salvation" — I did indeed take the point of that
well-worn text. Even today, I find it hard — no impossible!
— to understand anyone who works for some spiritual goal
in the remote future and is content to put off illumination
indefinitely. To me, this easy postponement always looks like
lack of seriousness, or else fear of self-loss, and escape from
the reality which is now or never.

My own childhood conversion was neither deep nor last-
ing. I'm glad to say that emotional, intellectual, and practical
difficulties soon intervened to save me from this exceedingly
partial salvation. The liberal influence of my day-school, stim-
ulating a growing interest in subjects such as drawing and
painting, nature study, geometry, and English literature (in
that chronological order); my very patchy private reading
(much of which had to be done in secret); and above all
the impossibility of living up to the standards of piety and
asceticism required by the Brethren — all combined to ensure
my fall from grace, though it was a fall in slow motion, with
painful ups and downs. Not until I was twenty-one and a
university student did I finally get around to leaving the
Brethren. And then the break was total.

It is understandable that very few of the Brethren's children
escaped as I did: the early influence was too binding. This
wasn't always a pity. A handful of the Brethren really did
come to a kind of illumination. They were truly converted and
thereafter lived a God-filled life. I remember vividly, from my
earliest childhood, three of the older men (two were Scottish
fishermen, annual visitors south from the Moray Firth) whose
exceptional spirituality was plain to me. A sweetness and

simplicity, a childlike joy and love shone in their faces and spoke through their gentle voices, and I adored them. Are the outward signs of true mystical experience ever lost on young children? No doubt the Brethren's prevailing eccentricity, drabness, ignorance, often morbid emotionalism, and above all their absurd fear and rejection of all outsiders — no doubt all this made up a heavy price to pay for the occasional saint in their midst. And a queer saint at that, deplorably narrow in understanding. But I certainly have reason for gratitude, for I came to recognise in such a one the supreme beauty of the Light that lighteth every man and the worthlessness of everything without it.

To my devout and lovable father in particular, and to the Brethren in general, I am surely indebted for more good things than I am apt to recognise — and certainly for a sense of the urgency and glow of the spiritual life, a sense of the suddenness and revolutionary quality of true illumination, and a sense of the wretchedness and futility of all things taken by themselves, as if they were self-luminous and independent of the Light. At least these curiously bigoted and single-minded Christians did know, and did manage to put over to me, that it is the best of bargains to trade all one has for the Pearl of great price, and that half measures will not do in religion. They even taught me how not to fidget in mind and body, how to sit still and think, so that eventually I could go on to teach myself how to sit still and *not* think. In fact, I can imagine many worse introductions to the mystical life than childhood among the Exclusive Plymouth Brethren, as they were more than half a century ago.

Intimations

Not everything, of course, can be attributed to nurture and environment: native tendencies are perhaps equally determining. In any case, much of what I now recognise as mystical experience in my childhood (or, let's say, experience with a mystical flavour, or with mystical promise) had little to do with the Brethren and wasn't overtly religious at all. Only now is its real significance emerging quite clearly. Here are some examples:

Colours were for me — they still are — a Revelation, a Mystery, a Bridge: not indeed all colours equally, but more especially the stronger and deeper ones, particularly when richly textured and blended. Certain shot effects, where a colour has overtones and undertones which seem to give it an additional dimension, a self-contained glory and intense *inner* fire; and, by contrast, certain waxy and metallic effects, where a colour has sheen and brilliance, a peculiar *outer* fire — these took my breath away. They showed up occasionally in paintings, more often in shut draperies and precious stones, and regularly in the glowing hues of such flowers as violets, pansies, petunias, zinnias (these above all), and more recently mesembryanthemums; and, again, in the wings of many birds and of such butterflies as the Small Copper and the Peacock. Especially transporting were certain colours blending into others, for example a deep orange shading off into greens and yellows: I can't see this combination even now, as in the paintings of Chagall, without feeling somehow exalted. Other numinously coloured objects included glass marbles or alleys, flags (the black-yellow-red Belgian was my favourite) and all stained glass. How admirable these miracles of colour were to me as a child I can't convey. In later years I have rediscovered their full splendour, their incommunicable message.

We lived in a tall, thin house high above the fishing harbour and the grey North Sea. One of my earliest and sharpest memories is stealing out of bed in the night to draw aside the blind and peep out — I think it was for the very first time — at the green and red harbour lights. The stars and the cold arc-lamps of the streets were wonderful, but nothing to the uncanny richness of those port and starboard lamps and their oily see-sawing reflections in the black water. From then onwards, coloured lights — the lights of buoys and piers and ships and traffic signals, firework fountains, the red and blue and gold neon signs of town centres shining in wet roads, the marvellous violet lights edging airfield runways, and especially the great cities of Europe and America seen from the air at night (actual heavens on earth, more thrilling than all the bejewelled Paradises and New Jerusalems thrown up by the pious imagination) — these weren't symbols of the only true Light, but its actual rays. Other things were more or less opaque or translucent to that Light; these were transparent to it, identical with it. They said and they still say more about the Nature of Things than all the books ever written.

Another poignant memory: on the beach, not far from our home, was an unclean and smelly old rubbish dump, a mound concealing glittering strata of coloured broken glass — for me, a mine of rubies, emeralds, topazes, sapphires. I filled my pockets with these sharp-sided gems, and when alone would gaze rapturously through them at so many private kingdoms — red and green and blue and yellow universes that nobody else knew about. But my treasury was soon discovered: my precious windows opening onto these monochrome worlds were dangerous, they would cut my pockets and me (as if I minded!); and so they were confiscated, and I was temporarily heart-broken.

Later on, I got the same rapture, the same sudden sense of revelation from certain kinds of music. None of the Brethren's hymns had any such effect on me, and no wonder. The words were either sentimental or dreary, and atrociously sung, or rather bawled — without any accompaniment: an organ, even a piano, was too "worldly". I'm thinking of odd snatches and phrases of music overheard in the street or at school. Here I must distinguish between "beautiful" music, of which there is a great deal, and "mystical" music, of which there is very little — in my experience. For me, mystical music isn't necessarily "good" music, and it tends to be repetitive, even monotonous, tum-tiddledy-tum-tum stuff; but it always carries a magnificent luminosity, an assurance of finality, of having come right Home at last. In some odd way, it explains everything perfectly, clearing up all the world's cruelty and despair, and releasing a mood which is neither sadness nor joy, but a profound satisfaction that seems to contain them both. My own particular collection includes parts of Stravinsky's *Petrushka* and Berlioz' *Les Franc-Juges*, a number of Schubert's and Brahms' last movements, much plainsong (the endings invariably), practically all the older and more nonsensical folksongs and carols, the occasional barrel-organ and honkytonk piece, and a few of the tougher and saltier pops. Edith Piaf's *Milord* is a good example which I'm driven to make. A Universe that comes up with sounds like these *has* to be a superlatively good Universe! They are as truly a clue to its real nature as the rare and splendid cactus flower is to the nature of the otherwise "repulsive" cactus plant and root.

This fairly sharp distinction between the beautiful and the

mystical in music is paralleled in painting. (Miro and Max Ernst and Chagall provide many examples of the truly mystical; Picasso very few.) And, but less noticeably, the distinctions are to be found in architecture. (Compare, for instance, the modern but numinous interior of Westminster Cathedral with the ancient but extrovert and businesslike interior of Westminster Abbey). But how far this distinction is a merely personal one, and whether (as I suspect) the line might be drawn in quite different places by others who do in fact make a similar distinction, I don't know. What I do know is that for me there are two kinds of phenomena — those which directly and clearly announce their Origin, and those which normally hide it. Often I have found myself, from childhood onwards, in a flood of unshed tears — tears of immense bliss over a few bars of poor or undistinguished music, or a splash of gaudy colour, which nevertheless uncovered all the hidden glory of the world. The glory can't be laid on; it doesn't reveal itself to order or always in the same degree, and what disclosed it yesterday won't necessarily do so today. But when it comes it's quite unmistakable, and death and all evil vanish before it.

A Zen Roshi recently remarked that what Western students of Zen most lack is the gift of tears. It's the hardness of our hearts, the tough and thick protective shell we've built around our tender egos, which must be burst through before any kind of Zen experience is possible. The onset of this sort of tears (not sentimental ones brought on by some conventionally tearful occasion, romantic or pathetic, which is apt to leave the mystic quite unmoved), may be one of the prerequisites (as well as a side effect) of the real merging of selves. These mysterious breakthroughs arrive unaccountably — a grotesquely masked ballet dancer, the lined face of a very old woman, poppies bending and shivering in the wind, a solemn small boy coming up with the answer in a difficult public quiz, a common act of kindness such as a child helping a blind man across the street, or my own father (it's one of my earliest memories of him) holding a penny to a bruise on my knee "to stop the pain" — almost any trivial scene may suddenly take on infinite significance and infinite beauty, and trigger off the explosion, the breakdown of our protective barriers. It isn't that these things are, in any ordinary sense, meaningful. The "Partridge in a Pear Tree" carol is "meaningless" to me, and "The Holly and the Ivy" almost so, but that doesn't prevent them from holding, on occasion, a "meaning" that is tremendous and even ultimate.

All the same, there was one very meaningful situation which did quite often produce a similar result; namely, the spectacle of great generosity and abandon. The first novels I ever read (secretly, of course) were *A Tale of Two Cities* and *David Copperfield*, and they stirred me profoundly. I remember standing on the station platform, only dimly aware of trains and people, lost in an ecstasy, glorified, breathless, after reading Sidney Carton's story (tritely sentimental to our adult, too-sophisticated minds) — the story of the dissipated, rejected lover pacing the streets of Paris repeating to himself, "I am the resurrection and the life: he that believeth in me, though he were dead, yet shall he live: and whosoever liveth and believeth in me shall never die," and then taking his rival's place in prison and on the scaffold. Again, after reading the story of Ham's similarly heroic death in *David Copperfield* I was for days quite transported. Much later, when I'd grown up, a number of classic films had the same devastating effect, among them *Kameradschaft, Thunder over Mexico, The Road to*

Life, *Monsieur Vincen*t, and *Paths of Glory* — films in which our shattered world was for me briefly oned, and men were no longer merely themselves. All through my life, I have been unable to witness or hear of these "breakdowns of separateness" in others without experiencing, sympathetically, a more or less catastrophic "breakdown of separateness" in myself. The other day, I came across the following account, taken from *The Yorkshire Evening Post*, of the kindness shown to a wounded British soldier by a German in Normandy in 1944:

> He carried me for 70 yards to the beach, then looked down at me, smiled, put a cigarette in my mouth, lit it, and put his lighter in my pocket. Then he took off his white shirt, tore it into shreds and dressed my wounds. Having done this, he kissed me, with tears in his eyes, and then walked away to attend to the other wounded.

Here, the meaning and the breakdown are extremely obvious, and there's no mystery — apart from *the* Mystery of love. It's as if the positive and negative forces in the world have to go on increasing until the limit is reached, and the potential so generated is suddenly released in a blaze of light; or as if the pieces of the universe were all tied together with strong elastic bands, and the further they are dragged apart the greater is the force bringing them together again, once they are let go. The more thorough the alienation of the self from the world, the more thorough the eventual unification.

Really and truly, everything's all right. Sometimes this perfection or all-rightness breaks through without any apparent cause or warning. My more poignant memories include many odd interludes of sudden elation and glory — racing home from school (but it was really flying a foot above the ground!) through the snow on a winter's evening, navy-jersey clad, the wind smacking my face, the deeply-shadowed streets deserted and the lamps all rayed and glowing; or strolling alone in the park on a Sunday morning after Meeting in summer, with a very ordinary brass band honking and tooting away in the distance; or in a sad mood gazing at a little red sunset cloud until there was only that cloud and no sadness and no gazer. The surprise and ecstasy of those not infrequent occasions were never far from cosmic wonder, from a sense of the superb mystery of existence. Quite frequently, I was an amazed child. I was astounded at the world and myself in the middle of it all. Everything was miraculous, and so much was so beautiful. Ah, what depths of awe, what delight!

It's true, of course, that I still didn't know Who I was — and yet not altogether true. There were stray intimations, unexplained emotions. Already around the age of eight I did notice, and thought very strange, the peculiar exaltation, the strong feeling of being ennobled and even deified, which came over me whenever I repeated to myself the text: "I am the resurrection and the life," or "I am the bright and morning star," or "I am he that liveth and was dead," and others of the kind. Naturally the feeling remained short of full Self-consciousness, and to have put it into a word like *deification* would at that time have amounted to unthinkable, unspeakable blasphemy. Nevertheless I knew, deep down, that this little "I" of mine and that great "I" — the "I" of those magnificent New Testament assertions — were the same "I". What's more, I can now see that some of the Brethren, my father and his father (also a simple and most beautiful character) among them, enjoyed occasionally the same foretaste

of the supreme identity — without beginning to suspect
themselves of it. In fact, don't we *all*, in our heart of hearts,
know very well just Who we are, though we spend our lives
suppressing — with, alas, almost total success in the end —
that one essential piece of information?

The Sick Soul

I suppose I must have been about eight or nine when I
began to exchange my early Paradise for someplace increasingly like Hell. In my case, it was the Hell of extreme — in
fact, morbid — self-consciousness. To the usual anxieties
of puberty (one's guilt feelings about sex were bound to be
exceptionally severe in such a home) were added a certain
native timidity and thin-skinnedness, unhappily combined
with more-than-average egotism. The result was a feeling
of being cut off, of being odd and at odds with everything.
The children of Exclusive Plymouth Brethren weren't much
at home in the world anyhow, and I was less so than most
of them. (A vivid recollection is of a walk in the town with
my father during the First World War. We were followed by
a large and furious citizen, twice my father's size, shouting
at him for his "cowardice". My father was, like most of the
Brethren, a conscientious objector to war service, and at one
time in danger of imprisonment on that account.) Anyhow,
whatever the combination of causes, I did in fact turn into
a painfully faced-up and bashful schoolboy, rarely unaware
of myself and the effect I supposed I was having on others,
incapable of looking most people straight in the face, and (at
my worst) afraid to walk down the main street, and going
instead by side streets where I was less likely to be recognised.
I was covered with confusion whenever, in company, attention

was drawn to me. To some degree this agonising disability remained all the while I belonged to the Brethren. It was only in my twenties that I outgrew it, and then slowly. Going back to college after vacation, or walking into a room full of people I knew but hadn't seen for some time, was still for me at twenty-one an ordeal more unnerving than any I have since suffered.

In one sense, I have got over this exceptional self-consciousness; in another, I never have — I'm glad to say. It's true that, as a young man, I often became interested in outside pursuits to the extent of forgetting myself in them for a time; and this was certainly a partial cure, or alleviation rather. The real cure was to come later, as *increased* and true Self-consciousness — as an awareness that's clear and not hopelessly confused, sustained and not erratic, experienced right here and no longer over there as if through others' eyes — in short, a Self-consciousness which has become no-self-consciousness, which is not forgetting one's presence but seeing one's absence. Looking back, I'm sure that the unhealthy self-preoccupation and shyness of my later childhood and youth were, in spite of everything, a sort of preparation (or even, for me, a necessary preliminary) for the insights which followed. I can't be sure, but I suspect it may be comparatively easy for a person who has been unhealthily self-conscious in childhood to become liberatingly Self-conscious, or truly Self-aware, in later life.

For me as a boy, to be so painfully self-aware was to be aware of my face, and of my nose in particular. I got the idea — an unfounded one — that my nose was large, misshapen, and red, and this caused me acute embarrassment. In fact, I believe this obsession (arising in part no doubt, from anxiety about sex) did to some slight degree actually change my appearance and begin to make itself true. For about seven years it plagued me so much that I sought the postal advice of quacks, and even began to look forward to the time when I would be old enough to afford plastic surgery. An absurd and miserable story not worth telling, except that I'm convinced my youthful preoccupation with my human features did in the end help me to see with unusual clarity my true features, my "original face", my "nose" in the Zen sense. (1) After all, the discovery that one is really faceless (for oneself) would naturally prove most welcome to one like myself, whose apparent face (for others) has given him so much trouble. (2)

Of course this worrying about my appearance was a symptom of a deep disturbance, of a basic alienation. I was a sick soul because (and my peculiar upbringing cannot entirely be blamed for this) I had become cut off to an unusual degree from my fellow creatures, and in the end from any sort of God or Reality. The Brethren, always at odds with the world, were at least certain that the Power behind the universe was wholly on their side; but when I began to doubt even His existence (and not merely His special concern for me as one of the Chosen) I was indeed isolated. When, at twenty-one, I finally got clear of the Brethren, I was in no condition to enjoy my freedom. I was a lost young man, quite alone in the world, with no faith in God or man, and almost none in myself.

One treasure I did retain. This exaggerated self-awareness was never wholly morbid, never quite unmixed with a spirit of inquiry. And gradually it grew into an insatiable curiosity about myself, a determination to find out, at any cost, who or what I really was.

Healing Gods

But first I sampled the usual "cures" for my sense of alienation, with almost no success. Trying to forget it all by immersing myself in my professional work was all very well, but beyond a certain point seemed a dreadful waste of precious time and mere escapism. That sort of ambition was very short-lived. The pleasures of unrestrained sex soon turned out to be anything but pleasurable — to say nothing of the harm to others. Ordinary hobbies, money-making, travel, social climbing, were tried and more-or-less-readily seen through. My upbringing no doubt helped here, contributing to my disillusionment. What did remain and flourish was ambition of a "higher" sort — ambition, at first, to work out an adequate philosophy of self-knowledge and to gain recognition for it, gradually giving place to an ambition really to understand myself, just for the sake of the understanding. But even this goal was perhaps as much a symptom of Self-alienation as it was the start of the real cure.

The true work of healing began inconspicuously, almost invisibly, and with no hints as to its outcome. Around the age of 23 I made a strange discovery — at that point a physical or biological one rather than a spiritual — *that I wasn't only a man, or really a man.* My proper shape wasn't at all human. My body didn't stop at my skin, but was extended, by means of artificial "skins" and "limbs" and "hands" and "sense organs", far and wide. And these extensions were, as included in my total Body, truly alive and immensely effective. Indeed I owed my manhood as much to them as to the flesh and blood at their core. I not only saw but actually felt myself enlarged, prolonged to new and often supersensitive extremities, grown up into that protean giant which man really is. The hammer was my hardened fist, pincers my lobster-claw. Saws, chisels, forceps, pens, brushes, all hand-tools whatever, were my genuinely human hands, each grown at the end of my arm to suit the occasion, and as quickly amputated. Clothes were my sloughable human skins; my house was the human body I grew when I felt like settling down and becoming a sessile organism; my car was the human body I took on when I wanted to outpace and outdistance the horse; a ship was myself grown seaworthy, as adapted to ocean life as any fish; a plane was this same human being flying, become a super-bird or *air*man; and so on. The bare human body, this soft and ineffectual nucleus, was by itself as incapable of any specifically human function, and as much an unnatural abstraction, as any of its appendages taken by itself. My working and effective organism was an indivisible whole, of which the great bulk wasn't flesh and blood, but every kind of software and hardware. This was what it was really like to be human.

At the time, I had no idea where this new (though as yet naive) estimate of myself would lead, and very little idea why it should so fascinate. The reason is now obvious. The living tool had started to break down the artificial, and quite imaginary, wall that had been building up between me and the world. It began the long work of re-uniting me with my fellow man and the Earth and the universe itself; it demonstrated in the most practical and concrete fashion, visibly and tangibly, how absurd was this notion of a separate individual, of a self-contained organism. It punctured this vessel, spilling its little life into the world's life, so that I no longer knew where I ended and the world began. No wonder the idea exercised a mysteriously powerful appeal. But at the time I was interested in the facts, not their therapeutic value; and

I'm sure the medicine would never have worked half so well if I'd thought that that was what it was.

As I followed up this clue — reading, meditating, drawing, (3) observing — the threads inevitably lengthened and ramified. Soon it became apparent that the living extensions of individual people were merged into common organs of a common life. For instance, houses were integrated into streets and suburbs and whole cities, whose immensely complex organisation was the true embodiment, the indispensable anatomy, of human life as it was actually lived. The city as a unitary being, or rather the entire network of cities and towns and villages spreading over the planet's surface, was alive, and moreover alive with *my* life. I was more truly the whole than part of this strange, plant-like creature. This was no doubtful hypothesis or article of faith, but obvious and quite inescapable. For, firstly, it was plain that, in almost all its day-to-day details, the kind of life I actually lived could only be lived this way, in and by this vast and complex Being. And nothing less complex, or less extensive in time and space, would do. Secondly, at least in my more expansive moods I genuinely felt enlarged, and just couldn't see myself stopping at my skin or coinciding with my merely personal goods. Thirdly, this same Being was clearly visible and audible (thanks to radio) as an ever-growing and ever-decaying reticulum. There it stretched below, feeding on the country and drinking at lakes and rivers and excreting its waste at convenient spots. Interesting rather than lovely to see by day, it came into its own by night — when it was often exquisitely beautiful and brilliantly luminous, and vocal and musical to excess. Evidently it was stupid and clever and highly intelligent all at once — exercising each "superhuman" function in its own peculiar way through its own peculiar organs, which were nevertheless *mine*.

So I wasn't really Douglas Harding. I was this marvellous Earth-enveloping Creature — still so splendidly unhuman — which almost everyone agreed to ignore. Indeed the mystery was not so much the creature itself (after all, its detailed anatomy and physiology and mentality were man's own know-how, his primary task) as the conspiracy of silence about it. I was, at this level, a very well-kept secret. And this was all to the good, because it forced me to discover the strange facts for myself. Self-knowledge can never be bought second-hand, anyway.

When this experience of Man or of my completer self as a vast living Creature first came to me, I happened to be living in London and working in the City itself; and it was a calming and heartening thing to feel myself one with all that rushing, important-looking, crazy commotion. I began to discover the precious knack of pacification by incorporation — by actually *becoming* the disturbance to settle it and render it void. Void of disturbance, not of meaning.

As religious or crypto-religious experience, this Man-consciousness was, so far, exceedingly incomplete; but somehow I made do with it for a few years while I had no other religion to live by. Perhaps it was in the end the stress of the Second World War years which pushed me on to discover higher gods than Man. Anyhow, it became increasingly obvious that this great Being was still far too small and a long way from being a living *whole*, a self-contained and independent Organism. In countless ways it relied upon other species and genera, whether directly or indirectly, and wasn't really itself without them all. So I concluded that, in fact, all Earth's living creatures, from bacteria to men, were only organs of one Creature. The true Organism was nothing less than the Biosphere, the planet's inhabited envelope, its living skin comprising all species and their living-space with Man as its co-ordinating network or nervous system.

This huge hollow sphere, it now seemed, was my true shape and more myself than any little human body could ever be. Again, though observation and reason and science itself all combined to point to this Super-organism, it was my heart which told me they were right and gave the final *imprimatur*. In the same way that I was perfectly sure I was all other men, I was perfectly sure I was all other living things and my division from them was a temporary illusion, a crippling act of self-alienation, a mistake. Cutting myself off from any sentient or insentient being, however nasty or foreign it might appear, was only wounding myself. For I *was* Life, and when I wasn't Life I wasn't feeling myself. I was to that extent dead.

From this point on, growth was much faster. The next step beyond Life was naturally the Living Earth. For clearly the Biosphere, or living Earth-skin, is utterly dependent upon the other strata — upon the air, rocks in all their variety, and water everywhere, and equally (though less obviously) upon the protecting upper layers of the atmosphere and the dense supporting core beneath. In other words, the universe is so constituted that nothing less than a heavenly body can live in it. It takes this kind of creature to grow to maturity and survive in the living-space of Space, and there isn't anywhere else to live. And it lives there *as a whole* — not as an inert space-platform to which we cling, or as a clod which has been somehow infected or infested with life, but as a unitary living being, even a divine one. I couldn't doubt that here was a Deity — call her goddess or devil or angel or what you like — for whom the evidence was quite overwhelming, and beside whom a man was a mere abstraction.

Nor could I doubt that the planetary life was all of it *my* life, otherwise it would have been opaque to me and any account of it impossible. In mind and in body I was Earth. To have been anything less would have been to forfeit life, perception, thought. And whenever I looked up at the sun and the planets, with all Earth at my back and dissolved into me, I vividly realised my planetary status. The idea that I was only human after all was utter nonsense. I knew with every layer of my being — I would have staked any number of lives on it — that I incorporated everything earthly down to the last molecule, and actually became this splendid goddess sailing through the heavens. I saw clearly that there was no life but heavenly life, and deeply to know this was to enter heaven and enjoy its peculiar peace and wholeness and health. When the choice was deification or death — and it was just that — how could I hesitate? But of course I'd already chosen, and it was my merely human life which was a fantasy and a dream.

But obviously again, this elevation to planetary status wasn't the end. When I looked up at the other stars, I wasn't merely Earth, but Earth's star, this solar system or developed sun complete with all the planets. And, of course, I'd never been anything else. For no man, or species, or biosphere, or even a living planet, could ever come into being or live for a moment without the sun which is the source of all their particular energies and the very heart of all terrestrial life. In fact, therefore, the smallest complete organism capable of coming to life and remaining alive in space was not after all a mere planet, but nothing less than a living star ringed by and including the planets which are its outer "organs". And even this divine life-form wasn't quite final. All the stars have proceeded from, and are still very much part of their parent galaxy, under whose ever-present influence they remain. And all the galaxies together are only organs of the total Organism, of that Whole which alone is altogether whole and altogether self-contained and alive.

And so at last I came to the conclusion that I wasn't all there, wasn't independent or a true individual, wasn't alive in myself, wasn't even existent, until I was absolutely Everything — this *indivisible* Totality. Whatever way I looked at myself, I found that in the end I could exclude nothing if I were to be myself — which is to say, my Self. I was the All. I had, through "gods", come to God.

In all this I just couldn't help myself. I was drawn by an unknown Guide, not led on by any conscious self which saw to the end of the path. It seems I had to take this twisting, halting, cosmos-scaling track. Looking back, however, I can now perceive the reason behind it. Others may do the work rather differently and use another language to describe it; but somehow we must all take on and take in the entire universe, or else go on being taken in by its seeming substantiality and opacity and independence of us, and so put off our liberation indefinitely. Obviously enough, the only way to go free is to escape from the prison of our surroundings, which in practice means getting outside them by outgrowing them, totally demolishing every wall and rampart to the outermost, by the simple expedient of incorporating it.

Later on, I was to learn that it is an essential Mahayana Buddhist doctrine — taken over by Zen — that Enlightenment is no private or merely human condition, but a truly cosmic one. It means turning mountains, rivers, seas, the earth, the whole universe, into the Self or no-Self, so that in the Enlightened One *all* sentient beings are oned, pacified, and voided of all individual selfhood. In other words, the Enlightenment of one is that of all, and to talk of an enlightened *man* is really nonsense. The only Liberation is liberation from being a man into being the Whole. Only the Whole is whole, wholly outside the world-gaol, alone, and free of any contents. As Eckhart says: "No soul gets to God until she *is* God."

The Inward Journey

According to the *Gandavyuha Sutra*, Bodhisattvas are in the habit of expanding their bodies to the ends of the universe. According to the *Mahaparinirvana Sutra* — another principal Mahayana scripture — the Tathagata does the opposite, too. He divides his great Body into innumerable bodies, extruding from it cities, villages, houses, humans. And according to the Zen master Shen-hui, one who sees the Unconscious (that is, himself as no-mind, no-body) is able to produce as well as take in all things. In fact, this teaching crops up again and again in all branches of Mahayana Buddhism. It isn't enough to incorporate and absorb everything, and make Light of it. One must also go into reverse and make something of it, until one is utterly emptied and the world is replete again. One must finally escape from the world-gaol by abolishing, not this time the prison, but the Prisoner.

So my tale of cosmic expansion was only half the story — the outer half which is quite unbalanced and misleading, if not actually meaningless, apart from the inner half which is a tale of cosmic contraction or withdrawal. I had to grow until

I incorporated all men, all living things, the whole physical world, and at the same time to shrink until I had shed in turn all vestiges of manhood, vitality, and materiality, and arrived at Nothing. I had to discover for myself, and in my own way, my ultimate smallness no less than my ultimate greatness.

In other words, I found that the question of my nature couldn't really be answered except by taking myself as I would appear to the honest observer at every range, however near as well as distant, and checking his findings over there against my own findings here at the centre. (4) The *retreating* observer saw me first as a man, then as a house, a suburb, a city, a country-covering and world-covering network, a planet, a star, and a galaxy, before I vanished altogether. And all he saw me to be, I felt like, and I needed to be. I truly was all these things. And my *approaching* observer, though travelling in the opposite direction, came by rather similar stages to the same conclusion. Properly equipped to see me clearly at ever closer range, he found first a man, then a head, an eye, a living cell, and particles of descending order, until at the point of contact I vanished once more into Nothing — into that same Nothing which I, too, found here at the Centre.

Thus I not only took science seriously, but (what is less easy) applied it to myself. For instance, I was not only raised to the level of the Lowest Common Multiple of all the living, namely the Biosphere, but also reduced to the level of their Highest Common Factor, namely the cell, the basic unit of life. I contemplated myself as a community of myriads of these tiny creatures, each living his own unique little life in his own fashion, without any thought of me. Douglas Harding had gone, and what was left was a kind of city-on-legs — a city without a king or even a mayor — miraculously parading the streets of that other city, the City of London. With what wonder and admiration I observed the perfect co-ordination of my citizens' efforts as one leg preceded the other, as my tongue wagged with such speedy precision, as my hands gesticulated and manipulated with an almost macabre efficiency — while, I, their lord and master, was content to stand aside and know myself a fiction! What right had I to put on airs anyway? If I imagined myself to be permanently or essentially human, how was it that in my own lifetime and not so many years back, I had been the inferior of the lowest mammal, the lowest reptile, the lowest fish, the lowest worm? Indeed I'd been an animal alongside whom my dog was a god in heaven, and the fly on the window a blessed angel. Everybody was agreed about the biological facts, at least in theory. Human embryology was no secret. But how many, when confronted with ovum and sperm or even with the comparatively human face of the foetus, would recognise themselves?

This extraordinary evasion and dishonesty, this double-think which enables us at once to believe and utterly to disbelieve, I found to apply almost as much to the physical as to the biological sciences. If I'm a man, I'm also a descending hierarchy of organs, tissues, cells, molecules, atoms, subatomic particles, and, in the end, virtually empty space. The idea that bodies are built out of solid and substantial bits, fitting compactly together, was of course exploded long ago. We all know that every seemingly solid object is really void, a space which is the locus of immaterial energies. But we're careful not to apply this supremely important piece of knowledge to ourselves. Only superficially, "with the tops of our heads" do we live in the 20th century. The rest of us is pre-scientific.

But I resisted this duplicity, this ostrich-like fear of the facts. I did what I could to bring myself up to date, and see myself as I really was to the unprejudiced observer — not as a solid or substantial body, but as innumerable views (almost all of them nonhuman) of that one unsubstantial Nucleus which is, in fact and in itself, Nothing at all.

Thus an empty and lifeless desert greeted me at the end of the inward journey. I found myself totally uninhabited. My subordinates had all left me. En route, I came across them in great numbers — limbs, organs, cells, and the rest — but I passed them by, and here at the goal no trace of them remained. In seeing the absence of my human body here, I saw also the absence of all my lesser bodies. I was their unicity, their clarification, indeed their Buddha. For he who sees through the illusion of his body as a whole, thereby sees through the illusion of every part of it. To borrow Zen master Hui-hai's terms, he liberates his internal beings even before they take shape in him. The infant and the animal are in a somewhat similar case. They are comparatively free from the illusion of having or containing or being bodies and parts of bodies. There remains the ordinary, common-sensical man who regards himself as a compact lump of very complex living matter, an elaborately structured solid, and pays a heavy price in suffering. As the masters insist, all his troubles stem from this body-idea. Such a man is specially liable to diseases which are malfunctions of his inferior bodies, their insubordination to the whole. Of course there are numerous levels of explanation, but I believe that the fundamental cause of our more "civilised" diseases is our failure to liberate our internal beings. It's as if our cells, cheated of their natural and happy innocence by having thrust upon them from on high the terrible illusion and anxiety of incarnation, fell sick. As animal innocence and enlightened vision are healthy all the way down the bodily hierarchy, so their opposites are unhealthy all the way down. The trouble isn't merely human, but involves every level. (5)

The trouble is cleared up directly we look. There came a time, indeed, when it was no longer a case of trying to see myself as I really was: my Nothingness here was perfectly obvious. The presence of the world about me entailed my own absence at its centre. Perception was necessarily of perceived things there and of no perceiver here — the two at once. The ultimate emptiness, that substratum-that-was-no-substratum which physics could only postulate or point to, I saw, and I saw that I was precisely that.

This occurred when, in the course of the cosmic explorations which I have just outlined, I had arrived more-or-less simultaneously at the goal of the inward journey — the empty Centre — and the goal of the outward journey — the full Circle, the Whole. Yet this seeing, in itself, had nothing at all to do with that two-way movement, or with any kind of preparation or thought or activity. Either one suddenly sees what one has always been, or one doesn't. It just happens, and nothing can be done to make it happen.

The Mandala

I doubt if I could have begun to make these discoveries, and brought them right home to myself, if I hadn't been continually helped along by visual aids. Among them were certain diagrams — they amounted to schematic self-portraits — which summed up for me, in a handy and wordless form, my cosmic constitution. By far the most fascinating and fruitful of these patterns was a very simple one, seen every time a stone is thrown into a pond. It consisted of a few circles drawn around a common centre and enclosing up to twelve annular "regions", though many embellishments were added as time went on.

At the pattern's unique and solitary Centre, I was the still Hub of the rotating Wheel of Life. I was the spaceless and timeless Point around which the spatio-temporal universe sorted itself out region by region — each region being distinguished by its contents and their behaviour, and ranging from the smoothly circling galaxies and stars and planets of the outermost regions to the frantically erratic particles of the innermost regions. All these regional objects, no matter how near, were labelled "there-then", and only the Centre was labelled "here-now" — a spot which has no room or time for anything. Yet in another sense it had precisely all the time and the room in the world. All things coincided with me, because this empty Centre was also full to overflowing and enclosed every region with all its contents, the whole packed universe. It was all clearly presented to me here and now. And when instead of merely looking *out* from the Centre, I imagined myself also looking *in* at the Centre, I found that viewed from each region I took on the status of that region. Thus, from the stars' point of view I was a star, from men's point of view a man, from particles' point of view particles, and from the Centre's point of view the empty Centre itself. (6) Each successive ring of the diagram (with what lay inside it) defined one of my numerous embodiments, subhuman or human or superhuman. It stood for that part of the universe which I had for the moment taken on and become, so reducing it to unity, transparency, emptiness, and hereness.

Conversely, each ring (with what lay outside it) defined that part of the universe which I had for the moment extruded and disbecome, so rendering it multiple, opaque, and at a distance. Thus, I was essentially the empty Centre, which nevertheless was capable of absorbing its regions to any extent whatever.

All this and very much more of the kind had become for me no mere cosmography or neat system of ideas and beliefs, but living and ever-growing truth deeply apprehended and enjoyed — thanks to the strange power of the Mandala diagram. Not that, when I first came under its influence, I had ever heard of Mandalas or Eastern meditation-diagrams. The pattern arose spontaneously from the depths of my own unconscious mind as the only fitting expression of what I was discovering myself to be; also as a key to further discoveries and an aid in the difficult task of turning from the outside world to the Centre. My Mandala was no merely intellectual device, even less was it a merely magical one. Though it kept up its irrational (or rather, superrational and even numinous) appeal for several years, it never became an end in itself out there instead of a means of realisation here. Its value throughout those years was that it helped to put me in my Place and keep me there. Even drawing the Mandala could serve this purpose, and I must have sketched it, with variations, thousands of times before it had done its work. In the end, it went out of my life as mysteriously and as abruptly as it had come in. Thereafter, whenever I was consciously centred, I *was* the Centre of the Mandala. I no longer needed any picture over there of what I saw myself to be here, or any map of the way Home.

Before I had done with the Mandala, I was thrilled to learn something of its universal significance for the religious life, its psychological potency, and its many picturesque forms. Though essentially a concentric pattern after the style of my own diagram (with or without four radii), squares often replace some of the circles, and all manner of embellishments are added. At the Centre appears some specially significant or sacred symbol, such as the face of God, Christ, an Eye, a Buddha, Shiva and Shakti embracing, the Vajra or diamond-thunderbolt symbol, or simply a Point. The whole diagram is felt to be mysterious, holy, magically potent, metaphysically revealing, an aid to concentration, or just fascinating for no particular reason. It is found in all cultures, primitive and advanced, from the Palaeolithic onwards, and in the West as well as in the East. In Tibetan Buddhism it reaches its greatest complexity, but Christianity can show some very elaborate examples. And its provenance ranges from the lowest to the highest human levels — from primitive magic and sorcery, through popular religion, to advanced mysticism. In short, it is built in, a universal ingredient of our deeper nature.

This isn't really surprising. If any picture at all is to play such a dominating role, how fitting that it should be no arbitrary symbol but instead a true sketch plan of what we are, setting forth so clearly and so simply — yet so adequately, compared with wordy descriptions — our true constitution. No wonder the Mandala has turned up in modern psychology, as the "unifying symbol" which the patient commonly produces from the depths of the psyche when his cure is well under way. According to Jung, the superficial or conscious mind cannot reach down to the healing unity symbolised by the Mandala. That mind is only a small part of ourselves and needs reuniting with our deeper mind, with the unconscious from whose abyss the Mandala emerges. The integrating effect of this emergence is said to be astonishing. With the powerful help of this self-produced device, the patient frees himself or herself from emotional and conceptual confusion, and is as if reborn on a higher plane. Of course, the psychologist as such isn't concerned with any metaphysical significance. What he finds is an autonomous psychological fact, an organ of the psyche which is as natural and perhaps as normal as any physical organ, and seemingly as important for wholeness and health. Certainly I can testify that in my own case this objectification of my deep involvement with all things and with No-thing, this spontaneous picturing of my true nature, reshaped my life. For me it did indeed prove to be the Key of the Kingdom, as in that most wonderful of all nursery rhymes:

> This is the Key of the Kingdom:
> In that Kingdom is a city;
> In that city is a town;
> In that town there is a street;
> In that street there winds a lane;
> In that lane there is a yard;
> In that yard there is a house;
> In that house there waits a room;
> In that room an empty bed;
> And on that bed a basket —
> A Basket of Sweet Flowers:
> > Of Flowers, of Flowers:
> > A Basket of Sweet Flowers.

In unpoetic language, my approaching observer, advancing through all my regional appearances, doesn't find the expected

man: the bed is empty. He is out, and has never been in. So
my observer backs away:

> Flowers in a basket;
> Basket on the bed;
> Bed in the chamber;
> Chamber in the house;
> House in the weedy yard;
> Yard in the winding lane;
> Lane in the broad street;
> Street in the high town;
> Town in the city;
> City in the Kingdom —
>> This is the Key to the Kingdom.
>> Of the Kingdom this is the Key.

I am a nest of boxes, with Nothing in the last box — but
that Nothing contains the whole nest. This is the meaning
behind all Mandalas, from the *kyilkhors* or meditation diagrams of Tantrism, the Golden Flower of Taoism, and the
elaborate emanation systems of Neoplatonism, to Dante's
Mystic Rose and St. Teresa's Interior Castle. (7)

The emergence of the Mandala from the unconscious into
the light of full consciousness was an essential part of my own
development, but not of everyone's. It is when religion takes
flight heavenwards (as in my childhood), when mysticism is
otherworldly and spirit can find no place in nature, that the
Mandala is most likely to appear as a partial compensation
or corrective. Like the body, the mind has its own means —
entirely beyond our supervision — of healing its wounds.

But where nature and spirit are not so divided, as for example in Zen Buddhism at its best, the Mandala remains in

abeyance. This everyday world, these common objects before us — this cypress tree in the courtyard, this bundle of flax, this rice-bowl, this shadowy nose, this faceless Face — set the scene of Enlightenment. In fact, it was my absurd attempt to escape from the ordinary and seek my good in the extraordinary, in some unlocated and airy spiritual realm instead of right here and now, which stood in the way of Enlightenment — the whole secret of which is simply attention to what's given. My precious diagram wasn't given, but it nudged and shoved until I stumbled into the true Mandala, the Great Mandala that is indeed given, namely my Self. Once I had moved in to occupy its unique Centre, and seen all its regions ranged around me alone, I needed the picture no longer.

What am I?
Unlike my looking-glass, the Mandala mirrored, though in outline, my true nature. It introduced me to myself. But one thing it could never do was explain me to myself, and order my universe so that the mystery was cleared up. On the contrary, the whole point of the diagram was its Centre, this focal and fundamental mystery which only grew deeper and deeper.

From boyhood onwards I have known, erratically but more intensely as the years went by, a feeling of cosmic wonder and astonishment, a sense of the improbability of anyone or anything whatever managing to exist. What an irregularity, what an outrage to common sense, what an impossibility "I AM!" Here's something indeed worth celebrating! Here's a considerable achievement on the part of Consciousness (or God, I AM, or whatever) — not merely to exist, but to be the only thing that exists, to have conjured oneself out of nothing, to be one's own Author, to be Alone. How deserving of my congratulations this someone or Something or Nothing is! This has always seemed to me to be *the* Mystery and Delight, the one matter for perennial awe and rejoicing. Next to it, all other mysteries seemed quite secondary, if not trivial. After the initial achievement of Being, anything can and probably will happen (what are a few billion universes more or less?) and all of it is in a sense an anticlimax.

In so far as I existed, I shared in this supreme mystery, and from an early age my surprise was increasingly diverted to myself. What am I? More and more it seemed to me a most miserable thing to live without asking this question all the time. So long as I found all other things remarkable, not to be taken for granted, demanding full investigation — all, that is, except this investigator himself — then surely I was hardly alive at all, let alone wide awake. What's more, I was missing life's finest pleasure — the intuition of an immense unknown, of heights and depths just glimpsed, of tremendous meanings just breaking through — and all mine, or inseparably bound up with my being.

What, then, was I? An infinite mystery, certainly. Nevertheless I felt sure that some kind of answer, if not a very profound one, could be discovered. My best chance of finding it seemed to lie in a combination of methodical study with direct self-inspection. From early manhood onwards, therefore, almost every moment I could spare or steal was spent in this two-sided effort of inquiry. I read every book — many hundreds of them, not all good ones — that promised to bear upon the real nature of man: or, more explicitly, upon the nature of man-in-the-universe and the universe-in-man, for evidently man by himself was an unreal abstraction. I filled shelf after shelf with books, drawer after drawer with notes — extracts, hunches, drawings, schemata, brilliant ideas, utter nonsense. And always the Mandala, in one or another of its varieties, served to organise and somehow unify all this chaotic material. Without such a framework on which to hang my findings, they would have remained a useless miscellany without shape or meaning, and the whole enterprise of self-discovery would have been impossible. In fact, the Mandala served me so well that it constantly suggested new lines of investigation and spurred me on to ever greater efforts. There were months when I worked all day and half the night, seven days a week, and scarcely ever left the house. I took five years off from my job for this purpose alone. If ever a comparatively sane man was obsessed, it was this one. I intended to find out what man was, or rather what I was (for it wasn't clear I was a man), or burst in the attempt!

From the very start what I found so remarkable was the huge discrepancy between the common sense view of me, the scientist's view of me, and my own immediate view of myself. No doubt all three were somehow valid, yet how were they ever to be reconciled. This was a question which appeared to trouble few enquirers, and I was obliged to seek my own answers. How on earth could I be at once an ordinary enough man, a republic of subhuman organisms, a cloud of particles, a perfectly empty space, and that space full of the universe? Again, contemplating these hands and feet busy at their tasks, how could I square what I found with what the physiologist and biochemist said was really going on here, in a physiological and biochemical world that so modestly hid itself from me — who, after all, was its proprietor. When dining, and I shoved foreign bodies into a hole in my head (actually, into a hole in a hole, a hole without anything holed), how was it

I failed to follow their further history, and couldn't even be sure they had a further history? Still more baffling was the scientist's account of how I was able to sense things. I just couldn't believe that an exquisitely scented rose, all crimson and yellow and flashing dewdrops, or that deep blue sky-vault, was a state of my brain. What had the chemistry of a handful of grey matter, boxed up in the dark and damp inside of an eight-inch ball, to do with the tremendously brilliant world which I found in its place? All of these questions were as difficult as they were vital and intriguing. Here again I found picture-making a great help. I tried to express these puzzles in sketches, or in strip-cartoons — childish looking, no doubt, but at least they enabled me to state the problem without verbiage.

Most captivating and compelling of all, there was the profound mystery of the mirror, of the face that was there instead of here. Long before I learned to take seriously what I saw where I saw it, I guessed that my looking-glass held the real secret, to understand which would be to understand myself. Just because it wouldn't easily part with that secret, it held me fascinated.

Such investigations — and these are only a selection — were far from being mere intellectual exercises. Their charm, their urgency, their long sustained importance for me, were independent of any possible answers, and certainly of the kind of answers that philosophy might offer. Looking back, I now see that they were, in fact, home-grown equivalents of Zen koans. For, like the koan, they led nowhere — nowhere but *here*. They were fictitious problems in the sense that they were incapable of solution out there, in the world of language and discursive thought. Their only solution lay in this all-dissolving Centre. No doubt that's why, in the end, they worked. And I'm sure that for us in the West these natural and native and contemporary koans of mine, with variations to suit individual needs, are far more effective than their oriental counterparts — so easily misunderstood — imported from another culture, and another age. Though despised, the best tools for our deepest self-investigation are all given, all at hand in twentieth century Europe and America. The job's difficult enough in any case, without supposing that we must all become Sinologists. (8)

Anyhow it was to this peculiar mixture of introspection and science and philosophy that I turned for light upon my real nature, and not to Chinese Ch'an or Japanese Zen (which were then little more than names to me), or to a religion of any sort. Science, at least, seemed to offer much positive and well-tested information, and it was comparatively uncommitted to any *a priori* answer to my key question: what am I? Absolute honesty in this enquiry seemed the cardinal virtue, and subservience to authority the cardinal sin.

Of course, the programme that with youthful enthusiasm I set myself was from one point of view quite impossible. The more physics, chemistry, biology, sociology, and astronomy I managed to absorb, the more I needed; and the deeper I dug in the fields of psychology, epistemology, and logic, the less hope remained of uncovering any real answers at all. From another point of view, however, this intense and long-drawn-out effort was a necessary one. I picked up a habit of one-pointed concentration. I enlisted, by conscious endeavour, the co-operation of those deeper layers without which no real work is done upon oneself; and certainly I found myself more vividly improbable, mysterious, and unknowable than ever. And oddly enough, this negative result, instead of frustrating, satisfied. I came to feel, rather than merely to know, my total ignorance; and it dawned upon me that this ignorance, paradoxically, was in fact true knowledge of my being. So the result of this largely intellectual work of mine was in effect the intellect's self-destruction. All at once, ever-growing complexity and doubt and confusion issued in a great simplification and clarity. Others may get beyond thought by not thinking — but not me.

Investigation or Training?

The genuine mystic may be a quite deplorable character. No wonder his or her strange gifts are always suspected by authority, if not condemned outright. For they have little to do with merit, and nothing to do with social usefulness and conventional good behaviour. In fact, it's notorious that they can lead to crazy and immoral excesses of every sort. If there are any moral prerequisites to mystical experience, they are childlike simplicity, open-heartedness, warmth, and a generous abandon — certainly not chastity, industry, reliability, prudence, unselfishness, piety, or even scrupulous honesty. The outcast, the rake, the mentally unstable, the madcap, are more likely subjects than the puritan, or the square and upright common-sensical upholder of the Establishment. On the other hand, the initial mystical insight, so undeserved and gratuitous, will never deepen and widen, and may soon disappear, if it isn't allowed to do its natural work of making over the whole man. Antinomianism is only the extinction — all acrid smoke and splutter — of the real fire that started it. Though the truly illumined man is never stuffy and may often scandalise, he necessarily loves everybody. And before too long this universal charity must come out in his behaviour, even to the extent of his becoming a quite decent, practical, useful citizen. Only the embryonic or imitation mystic *remains* an unsatisfactory man.

As for myself, my first teenage attempt to be "good" and "religious" (this was after I was "saved") was my last. Since then I've never even tried. It's true that my reading as a young and fairly young man included most of the standard works of Christian mysticism along with a few Indian scriptures, but I was far from religious. I wasn't even virtuous. My effort of self-enquiry was a search for knowledge, not for any kind of salvation, merit, or spiritual attainment. I didn't worship, or pray, or practice any kind of meditation or discipline, except as these arose naturally out of the work itself. As for behaviour, I was only average, and on occasions well below average. I spare the reader any detailed confession, but assure him that I speak the truth.

Nor can I pretend that my aim of self-discovery involved no self-seeking whatever. I doubt whether, if I had been a Crusoe with a vast library but no hope of rescue and recognition, I would have worked so hard or with anything like such a sense of urgency. Of course I told myself that I must communicate, must help others by recording and publishing the results of my enquiry, and that this was no bad motive. And perhaps in fact this was no worse than other respectable ambitions, such as making a fortune, or climbing to the top of one's profession, or trying to become a saint. However, it did have one advantage over many other forms of egotism. From the very start it incorporated its own self-destroying device, its built-in time-bomb with the fuse all set for an explosion one day. For the more I sought my real Self the more I saw it as void, beyond all seeking and knowing, all improvement or deterioration. And the more I sought my pseudo-self, that empirical ego whose vanity was flattered by the very seeking, the more I saw it as something which must be humbly accepted for what it is — by definition selfish, by nature beyond any radical reform. This was what it was like to be a man; and rebellion against the inevitable human condition could at best only be repression, at worst suicide, and in any case no way to Enlightenment. The essential thing, then, was to go on seeking to *understand* rather than change myself. Any worthwhile improvement would flow naturally from the clear perception of my real nature as void, and detachment from my false nature as body. In short, this method of intense self-investigation still seemed to be the right one for me, impure motives notwithstanding.

Certainly it was interesting, eventually, to learn that the Indian sage Ramana Maharshi always advocated self-enquiry as the one infallible and direct means of Liberation. He taught that as soon as we start asking the question "Who am I?" the process of inner transformation is set up, though its goal — involving complete detachment from the body — may be long delayed. Again, it was particularly interesting to learn that the essence of Zen training is earnest enquiry into one's self-nature, without ever letting go, and to the point of obsession.

Of course my own way has been very different from any Eastern one. For this no apology is needed. If we Westerners, instead of feebly abandoning our peculiar objectivity and our comparative freedom from pious axes to grind, were to have the courage of our virtues and push them to the limit, then we should find ourselves at the heart of traditional wisdom.

To take seriously what's given, and only that, is all that's wanted — a simple enough task, East or West. In fact, too simple, and (for that very reason) extremely hard.

But even in the West, few of us begin by looking to see what we are. More often it is unhappiness which drives us to look for help to a particular religion, whose teachings must be learned, understood, and applied. Enquiry into the religion comes first; enquiry into the self comes later, as part of instruction and practice with a view to spiritual growth and the end of suffering. But this self-investigation can't begin to succeed until it's found so interesting that it is pursued more and more for its own sake, and not for any good it might do us. No doubt absolute purity of motive is a counsel of perfection best forgotten until it comes unbid as part of the goal itself. Possibly a few religious geniuses may from an early age avoid this contradiction altogether. They may egolessly enjoy the infinite reaches of the present, unobscured by spiritual or any other ambition or by the memory and anticipation which are the ego itself at work. But the rest of us have to put up with somewhat mixed motives until we actually *see* there's nothing here for them to attach to, and then we're at last entirely disinterested and couldn't care less about our Enlightenment.

As a matter of fact, people of different temperaments set off along different paths. Traditionally, three main routes are described — the Way of Works or selfless service to one's fellow creatures, the Way of Devotion to the Deity, and the Way of Knowledge of oneself. How far the first and the second of these Ways can take us, and at what stage all three are merged into one supreme Way, are questions that don't concern us here. My only point is that the essential feature of all three Ways is a certain objectivity, a genuine interest in what's so, a deep concern about man or God or the Self-nature as they really are. In so far as these good works and pious devotions and penetrating enquiries aren't pursued for their inherent and present value, but as religious exercises in order to win Enlightenment one day for oneself, whether in this life or in a hundred lives' time, they will surely fail in their object. For there's no fourth path, no Way of Practice, which is interested not in the subject-matter itself but the method, not in man or God or the Self-nature but in how these can add to our stock-pile of merit and our beautiful spiritual status. To those of us who pine and hanker after this blind alley, Meister Eckhart shakes a warning finger: "Thou art not seeking God merely. Thou art seeking for something with God, making a candle of God." And if this is a way which some are compelled to try, then they will find it's going due south to get to north, and every mile of it adds at least a mile to the Great North Road.

Actually, there's no Great North Road, or any Way. There's no progress along any path. All spiritual success stories are pure fiction. Most of us would be much better off if we'd never heard of that enchanting but illusory idol called Enlightenment, that mirage which flickers and gleams with false light at the end of our chosen Way. For real spiritual success is total failure, the defeat of all our ambition (which isn't a scrap better for being spiritual ambition). It's the realisation that there's absolutely nothing to be achieved, that all's well here and now, that we've never for an instant left the goal we're striving to reach one day. Our bondage isn't failure to *win* our liberation, but to *see* it. In fact, it's our aim that stands in the way of its realisation. It's our anxiety to arrive at perfection in the unreal and unrealisable future which hides the Perfection which at this very moment is staring us in the face.

I'm no believer in practice for its own sake or by itself, and have never done any. Either I enjoyed the work primarily (I don't say only) for its own sake, or gave it up. Moderate appreciation wasn't enough. It had to be seen as very good and valuable work indeed — in my not-at-all-humble estimation — if interest was to be sustained. My earliest nursery paintings, my earliest doggerel as a boy, my earliest and crudest philosophical essays as a young man, never looked beyond themselves. They were the end, the final masterpieces — until they were finished and promptly scrapped. The very first house I designed (I'd been studying architecture for one week) was intended to be an improvement on all houses to date! Call it bumptiousness, cockiness, over-confidence, running before I could crawl, total lack of patience, or a tremendous zest and appetite for the riches of the present moment and to hell with the future (and it was all of these), or what else you like; it happened to be my way, the only way I got things done at all. I never could stick at anything that wasn't somehow valuable at the moment of doing it. And I could stick for years on end, without a day's intermission, at the thing which held me fascinated from instant to instant — my own true nature.

Paradoxically, this inability to practise was for me the best and only possible practice; this neglect of the future was the one thing that secured it. Really it's impossible to be under-confident about the future and over confident about the present. Liberation, enjoyment, everything worthwhile, is now or never. When I got bored and disheartened and anxious, as occasionally I did, this was to me a sure sign that I'd strayed from the path, or rather from the goal. For the

only true Way is so short it starts where it ends. Soto Zen
has rightly insisted that the only effective practice isn't practice at all, but realisation. True *zazen* isn't sitting-meditation
with a view to satori by and by, but present seeing into the
self-nature. There's no future in it, and no past either — in
fact, those are the whole trouble. *Bodhi*, as Hui-hai declares,
is ours the very moment we decide it *is* ours.

The Rinzai Zen sect isn't unaware of these truths. Rinzai
(Lin-chi) himself taught that practice with an end in view
doesn't work. There's no goal, nothing to be sought, and if a
man thinks he's found anything, it certainly isn't Enlightenment. And even one or two Christian mystics had some sharp
things to say about spiritual training. Of the Beatific Vision,
Ruysbroeck says: "To it none can attain through knowledge
and subtlety, neither through any exercise whatever." Only
the present satisfies. Nothing's wanting here, nothing's to be
done — except to recognise that fact. Enlightenment can only
come when we no longer want it, or desire anything at all.
Let's not confuse the thing itself with its products. We shall
never learn to see our Self by practising or working for the
consequences of that seeing, whether they be concentration,
calm, compassion, detachment, or freedom from complexes.
Only let us *see*, though at first so briefly; only let us see *now*,
and all the rest will follow quite naturally. Otherwise, nothing
rings true or smells sweet.

Look Who's Here
My long but joyful work of self-investigation has never
involved any deliberate spiritual discipline. And I still find
that my way is to avoid set times and topics and postures of
meditation, and simply attend to the Void as it's given, and

as happens to be convenient. This presence of mind is very natural and down-to-earth; in fact, it only comes when thinking goes. It's so natural that from outside it's unobservable (unless perhaps the observer knows what to look for), and can therefore be enjoyed anytime and anywhere. Also it's not hard; if effort is needed, it's rather the effort to hold effortlessness. It comes when invited and often may arrive uninvited, and may stay for perhaps half an hour with little attempt to hold it. Contrary to expectation, withdrawal from ordinary life is no help; actually, it tends to hinder. For the purpose of this awareness, open eyes are better than closed eyes, sitting up is better than lying in bed, walking in the garden is better than sitting indoors, and walking in the crowded street can be best of all. After a time it becomes the easiest thing in the world to cease seeing one sort of person, and instead to see two sorts everywhere: the plural, headed, solid bodies walking by, and the singular, beheaded, empty body floating here — this absent presence which feels so transparent and unsubstantial that it's almost a wonder people don't walk clean through it. (9)

The more one wears the cap of invisibility the better it fits. One gets so used to impersonating a gust of wind blowing down the street, or a cloud hovering and gliding above the pavement, that it seems more natural than mere walking (as indeed it is) and much less effort. And the secret of this magic — this combined vanishing and levitation trick — is an open one. Once learned, there's nothing to it. One has only to turn around (so to say) looking in as well as out to see that there's no pedestrian here, that this piece of the pavement is quite unoccupied. This doesn't mean that one is dangerously unconscious of what's going on. Quite the reverse. The chances of getting run over are lessened, because one's thoughts are no longer elsewhere. In the last resort, all unawareness of the present Void is absentmindedness, and more or less dangerous. Equally, when one is driving, this mindless attention can be an enjoyable safety precaution. One sees that a car driven by nobody is well driven. Even when reading or writing or talking, this peculiar awareness — this vivid seeing of the Void, through what arises in it — isn't really difficult. In fact there comes a time when it's practically impossible in most circumstances to keep one's head; it just won't stay. Even so there are occasions — when one is doing hard physical work, perhaps — which are apt to prove Void-obscuring, but all the same an undercurrent of awareness comes through.

There's no mistaking this condition for ordinary presence of mind, or attention to the task at hand. It's attention to the Void behind and containing the task in hand, and therefore an utterly different experience. An indescribable quality (clarity, brightness, simplicity are only its metaphors) marks it off as unique. It has a quiet joy of its own which knows neither agitation nor boredom. No chore seems a waste of time, no street mean and dreary, no man repulsive, nothing common nor unclean — a gentle but unmistakable light bathes all. Meanings and uses go, distances fold up, and colours glow strangely. Merely to be is the greatest happiness.

There are physical indications, too, which one noticed at the beginning. These include a curious limpness, as if one were a doll whose sawdust had just run out; a drooping of hands and arms, and a relaxation of facial and neck muscles; a slowing down of breathing, with rather deep exhalations held for longer than usual; sometimes almost a ceasing of the breath; and a stillness — even a fixity — of the whole body. At the same time there's a feeling of youth, freshness, well-being, and great reserves of energy. (10) Sometimes the physical counterpart (for instance, in an emergency) precedes the mood; at other times the mood (for instance, when it's deliberately evoked) brings on the physical counterpart. But these distinctions become less real when a settled state of emptiness, which is neither physical nor mental, is increasingly enjoyed.

In all this it is vision which dominates. The other senses play much less part. This is largely due, no doubt, to one's particular temperament and occupation. But it's not for nothing that so many of the metaphors of mystical religion are derived from sight, and that Zen monks, even at the highest level, meditate with open eyes. Nevertheless, hearing is for some the main door to the Self. They hear without ears the Silence behind all sounds, rather than see without eyes the Invisible behind all sights. In Chuan-tzu's terms, they hear Hearing rather than see Sight. Turning inwards, they listen to the Self-nature. By which sense-door one enters, however, is merely incidental. All that matters is that somehow one gains access to the inner Void, yet without losing touch with the outer world. For the mere Void, the inner world by itself and unexpressed, Nirvana without Samsara, is vacuity, a false abstraction, to be lost in which is the trance of death.

Getting in is one thing, living there another. Just as it isn't enough that our emptiness be *understood* — it must be vividly *seen* (or heard) — so it isn't enough to understand and see our emptiness; it must also be deeply felt. It's as if the body were voided downwards. Unlike the Cheshire Cat who disappeared tail-first, this is diving head-first into the sea of Nothingness.

We begin by understanding it in words, with the very tops of our heads (so to say) or in the captive balloon just above our heads. Then we see it, wordlessly, when our heads and necks melt away. Finally, we feel it, much lower down, as a great emptiness at the pit of the stomach, a totally hollow sensation, an experience of complete vulnerability, letting go, relaxation. This is the really profound acceptance of our nullity, when down here in the belly there is no longer anything to react at all. Then we're never hurt nor flattered nor grieved, but content to let things happen as they will.

Of course, until all three modes of realisation are one, and lived simultaneously, none of them really works. How can we understand our absence, much less clearly see it, if we're still present enough to be hurt, if enough of us remains here to be depressed when we're attacked, or elated when we're praised? The belly is the last hide-out of the retreating ego, and it isn't enough to send down a chaser; we ourselves must get down to it and be it. Descend from the bright upper regions of the conscious and preconscious to the darkness of the unconscious, and it's all instantly lit up and emptied — for where "we" are is Nothing whatever. If seeing our Original Face doesn't include descent into our Original Belly, then our seeing is shallow, and has only begun its profound work. The true vision penetrates all levels and regions, sees through everything, and leaves no hiding place or toehold here, or any shadow of one.

Conclusion

I have told the story of my heart — and head. It isn't for imitation. Each of us must find out by experiment his own best method of working, or absence of method, and as far as possible refrain from judging others. On the whole, words are unprofitable, and argument positively harmful. One can talk a person's head off without loosening it by a hair's-breadth — unless they happen to be already on the point of losing it, in which case one's help is a very small thing indeed.

In spite of my best efforts to avoid pious jargon and learned humbug, I've made it all sound too queer, too difficult, too complicated. That is THE lie! The only difficulty is the blinding obviousness and simplicity of this thing. We just can't believe it's as easy as that, so we make endless difficulties and assiduously trip ourselves up. This Great Work is the lightest work in the world: it's done. This Seeing can't be overlooked: it's seen in all seeing. This Void is our life: we can't get out of it. It's we who insist on standing in our own light. And the older and more "spiritually advanced" we are, the more oriental bogies and occidental hobgoblins we are apt to rig up between ourselves and Enlightenment. Year by year we grey-heads seem more determined that everybody — and especially our juniors — shall be cheated of that rightful Heritage which we've somehow missed in spite of all our devoted labour.

It's nonsense, evil nonsense, to say that long and weary years of discipline are needed before we could hope to see this thing. On the contrary, unless we *begin* by seeing, the years will very likely be wasted. But after seeing — why then fifty or seventy years will be all too brief a time to deepen our realisation, to really get down to it, to enjoy its beauty. "Having once got into it," says Eckhart of the habit of God-consciousness, "no life is more easy, more delightful, or more lovely".

I implore you to forget anything I've said which could

put you off, which could discourage you. There's nothing to prevent you seeing Who you really are, totally, through and through, before you get to the end of this paragraph. If you think you just aren't the type, let me whisper in your ear the fact that Soto Zen masters have estimated that nine out of ten people are capable, in this very life, of Realisation. Let me add that anyone who is at all stirred by this book is likely to be among the nine. But enough of this talk. Satori in all its degrees, Enlightenment, Liberation — these grand words applied to you and me are, frankly, nonsense. Spiritual attainments are quite mythical. There's no end to our disabilities, any one of which would be enough to bar us forever from Enlightenment. Our case is absolutely hopeless. However, this is no cause for alarm. It's all peripheral. Right here the sovereign Centre reigns. Here is the one that exists Alone and alone Exists, though infinitely beyond aloneness and existence. Who could attain except ITSELF, and what need to attain?

References

1. Instead of the Zen term "original face" or "face", the term "nose" is sometimes used as in the following *mondo* from *The Transmission of the Lamp*:

> Monk: Before my parents gave birth to me,
> where was my nose?
> Master: Even after you are born of your parents,
> where is it?

2. Milarepa (1040 — 1123) seems to have had similar trouble at one stage of his life. Reasoning that if the male organ

needed covering, then the nose (a similar protuberance) needed covering, and he proceeded to make a garment for it.

3. In fact, much of my meditation at this time was drawing. Throughout the task of self-investigation, I found picture-making much more helpful than word-spinning. It ranged from mere diagrams (indicating, for instance, the regions or levels of self and not-self) through portraits of little men with big heads busy enquiring into their mysterious natures, to faithful pictures of human organs, cells, foetuses, and embryos. More important, I found myself drawing, as accurately and frequently as possible, all I could make out of Douglas Harding — his hands, feet, and mirror-heads, with nothing at their centre.

For me, drawing was the beginning of seeing, and I think that I would still be blindly groping in the dark if my pencil hadn't acted like a scalpel to remove the cataract from my Eye. I can't sufficiently recommend this simple little surgical instrument. The person who goes on drawing what he or she sees is liable one day to *see* what he or she sees.

4. Thus Kahlil Gibran: "How could I have seen you save from a great height or distance?" And, better still, the Guard who observed Alice first through a telescope, then through a microscope, and then through an opera glass.

5. There's nothing pale and sickly about Enlightenment; it's our natural, normal, healthy state, robust and energetic. Master Hsu-yun, who died in 1959 at the age of 119, was even in his later years capable of walking thirty miles a day in hilly country, leaving his young disciples far behind. There is much

evidence that unusual resources are available to the one, like Hsu-yun, who sees himself as void through and through. His last message was: "Vow to achieve the perfect understanding that the illusory body is like dew and lightning." As *The Secret of the Golden Flower* so truly states: "Strength is in visioning the empty."

6. I called this the *Law of Equality* — equality of mutual observers. D.E. Harding, *The Hierarchy of Heaven and Earth: A New Diagram of Man in the Universe* (Gainesville: University Presses of Florida, 1979), pp. 24, 42 — 4, 65, 81, 121, 152.

7. The last of these is particularly interesting. St. Teresa pictures the soul as a perfectly transparent diamond or crystal containing many mansions ranged around God at Centre. Ordinarily, she says, we live in the outer courts, ignorant of what lies within. But when, by prayer and meditation, we turn our attention towards the Centre, we find our Interior Castle to be immense. As we progress through its concentric mansions, a delicious sense of interior recollection comes over us. Our breath seems to cease. We feel quite bodiless. At length we know a self-forgetfulness so complete that we appear not to exist at all. There remains only the empyrean heaven, a dazzling cloud of light, in the very Centre of our souls.

No doubt the Saint intended all this to be taken as an elaborate parable, an easily grasped picture in space of spiritual things which are out of space. That need not deter me from locating her concentric courtyards out there in the regions where I am in turn more-than-human, human, and less-than-human — and locating their Centre here where I vanish, and

Reality shines alone and unhindered. The Interior Castle is valid as a religious symbol because it is also (in spite of its designer's conscious intentions) a diagram of what I am in actual fact, visibly, in this very place and at this very moment. Whether I move into the next room, or go out for a walk, I take this immense Castle with me everywhere.

Its outer courts are always ranged about me over there, region by region, and I am always safe Here at the bright Centre.

8. To some, the seemingly intellectual content of these contemporary "koans" may appear alien to Zen, with its celebrated irrationality and spontaneous nonsense. This haywire element in Zen has been much exaggerated in the West, partly because it seems to justify flippancy and laziness. Also, there are real difficulties in understanding — our ignorance of the language and cultural background of the *koans* makes many of them sound more absurd than they really are. Zen is not a superior brand of surrealism. "There is in it", wrote D.T. Suzuki, "something that may be termed cold scientific evidence or matter-of-factness…That Zen masters were invariably students of philosophy in its broadest sense, Buddhist or otherwise, before their attention was turned to Zen, is suggestive."

9. Japanese *do* or "ways" include the practice of the Void when engaged in ordinary household duties. One method is for the student to draw a line down his body, from the bridge of his nose to just below his navel, and think of it as a line of light until the rest of the body vanishes. He then goes about his task, concentrating on the central line.

10. "When I see it," says Hildegard of Bingen (1100 — 1178) about the Living Light, "all weariness and need is lifted from me, and all at once I feel like a simple girl and not like an old woman."

* * * * *

ESSAY TWO

THE MYSTICAL VIEWPOINT: AUTOBIOGRAPHY OF A SIMPLETON

1. THE NAME OF THE GAME

In this introductory chapter I aim to set out in some detail what I'm up to here, and what my reader is in for. This way, you will know from the start what this book is about, and how it manages to combine a treatise on mysticism with the life-story of a man who isn't so much weak in the head as off it altogether. Thus putting us both well and truly into the picture. You in my picture, me in yours.

My first idea was to call the book *Varieties of Mystical Experience*. Not an inappropriate title. But it turned out that an American writer had beaten me to it. And a good thing, too, because the title I've settled on is much more to the point. So much so that I can't do better than devote this chapter to an explanation of what I mean by each of its terms: 1. The Mystical... 2. viewpoint. 3. Autobiography... 4. of a Simpleton.

1. The Mystical...

This is a tricky one. You could say that mysticism is a sustained and progressively futile attempt to scrut the Inscrutable, in which you know less and less about more and more till you know Nothing — to your great delight. A singularly unprom-ising way, you would think, of structuring the interval between cradle and grave. By itself, however, this definition won't do at all. It tells only half the story. Yes: there's a sense in which mysticism cultivates mystery, but there's also a sense in which it weeds out all mystery — and emphatically all mystification

— with a ruthless hand. At Core, the mystical experience
is clearer than Clarity, closer than Home, more certain than
infinity being bigger than zero. And, at the same time, more
gorblimey ordinary than fish and chips and a pint of bitter.
It is more transparent and accessible, more prevalent and
necessary — and certainly purer — than the air we breathe.
And more basically obvious, and obviously basic, than the
fact that you and I — against all the odds — have occurred,
that we actually exist. And — largely by reason of this match-
less immediacy and intimacy — it is the most overlooked
and undervalued of those attainments which distinguish us
humans from animals.

And, when not neglected, a cock-shy. Spell it misty-schism,
and raise a condescending grin, if not a derisory haw-haw. Yet
the truth is that we have here the keenest of cutting edges and
a model of precision. In contrast to so-called common-sense
— as well as so-called mystical flights from that same common-sense — mysticism proper is the relentless enemy of
vagueness in general, and of spiritual obfuscation and waffle
in particular. (The improper and bogus sort, defecting on a
huge scale to the other side, positively *revels* in the stuff.)
Certainly, the only varieties of mystical experience we shall
have time for here are uniquely down to earth, grounded as
only the highest skyscraper has to be grounded. The sober
fact is that, though advertised to be the scattiest of humans,
the true mystic or seer is the most sensible and most practical
and together of them all, the most with it, the most realistic
by far. Above and below all, he is the most natural.

And therefore the most assured. Or, let's say, Self-reliant. I
am being mystical when, daring at last to be my own authority,
I take *what it's like-being-me-here-and-now* seriously enough

to spare it just a little attention. I am a practising mystic when at last I'm inquisitive enough to look at, and humble enough to take, what's actually given — given to this First Person Singular, present tense — without immediately and compulsively tearing and twisting and trimming it to fit the socially-laid-down templates. I am living the mystical life when I cease being so goddamned naive, so eager to take those templates for the last word and gospel truth and the measure of all things.

For mystical, then, read straightforward, game-free, transparently honest, wide (oh so wide!)-awake, not easily conned. With plenty of surprises to follow — and rich prizes too — as we shall see. Just to begin to live this way is to turn upside-down everything I'd been told about myself. All of it. Not just the upholstery and optional extras of my life but the vehicle itself — thereby (believe it or not) making it twice as roadworthy. And by the same token — not surprisingly — upending the whole landscape, the world as viewed from this windscreen of mine. It, too, becoming mystical through and through, is transfigured. Radically, and in many unforeseeable ways. I promise.

In practice, the mystical life is of-a-piece, un-choosy, all-inclusive. Which means that in this book I shall feel free to touch on, and sometimes delve deep into, matters which are normally put down as the very opposite of mystical, matters which are ostensibly as trivial and mundane and crude as they come. So be prepared to read about (I'm taking a wildly random sample) how to prepare carrots, and make a passable after-dinner speech, and keep that bank balance out of the red, and enjoy hot buttered toast and Seville (I say it has to be Seville) orange marmalade. Also, be prepared — in the

interest of truth as against fantasy — to find yourself enter-
taining potbellied angels, and seriously investigating what
drains have to do with love. Just at the moment, I can't think
of any mortal thing that mysticism, within the meaning of the
act, leaves untransformed. And certainly nothing it leaves out.

Yes, there's fun to be had here, all right. But all the more
amusing because it's not fun for fun's sake, not funny-man
stuff. True, the mystical is lighter than sunlit mountain air, but
it's also more weighty and substantial than the deepest granite
bedrock. Its smile is never far from tears, or its tears from the
laughter of the heart. It's about a Beauty that drenches and
dissolves the beholder, that turns all beauty into prettiness and
ugliness into its foil. It's about a love so unconditional that
it leaves no one and nothing unloved. It's terribly shocking,
and shockproof. It's the highest and the lowest, the alpha
and the omega, the bright and morning star — and quarks
and strangeness and charm...

So wholehearted and comprehensive and hard to pin down
is mysticism. Not so the mystical...

2. ...viewpoint

I shall not even try to define this term and my use of it here.
There's no need. I have a surer way of conveying my meaning
— of getting it across to you absolutely — provided you will
do the little thing I now ask. Which is to *point to your face*...

...and make quite sure what (if anything) it looks like right
now... Keep looking in at what you're looking out of... for
(say) ten seconds.

Well, this is the mystical viewpoint.

See what that forefinger of yours directs your attention to.
Take it for what it manifestly is at this moment, not what it

means to you, not what you happen to think or feel about it, or have been taught about it. Go by present evidence. Just don't lie to yourself any more about what the scene is at the very centre of your scenic world. About what, at long last, you can see has been waiting there unobserved all the while. And about what hasn't. To be wrong about this is to be wrong about everything. It is to suffer from the very worst form of heart disease. The apple of your life is no sounder than its core.

I repeat, this is the mystical viewpoint.

Not a preview of it. Not a part or an aspect or even an instance of it. Not a beginner's impression of it. Not any sort or version of it, but the real McCoy, the whole works, the genuine article, the thing itself delivered in tip-top condition to your doorstep. In fact, aren't 'thing' and 'article' just about the worst words for it? And did you ever lack it? Just try looking out of something else!

How different is what you *are* — what you are for yourself at zero feet from what you *look like* to others at (say) ten feet! What a contrast there is — and has to be — between your never-changing Reality and all the ever-changing regional appearances it's giving rise to. How little resemblance between the immaculate nonhuman Front you present to yourself, and the all-too-human front you present to others. Between what some mystics call your Bright and Charming Original Face (which, as faceless, takes on all faces, and features the wide world) and your acquired face (which, as altogether faced up and face-full, features only its own solitary and narrow self).

Could the incompatibility, the great gulf fixed between what they say you are and what you see you are, be any deeper and wider than it plainly is? Could the confidence trick that tells you that you *are* what you look like be a dirtier trick or one more fallen for? Or easier, once your attention is drawn to it, to rumble?

And here's some more news for you, and about you personally, which I hope you'll take as wonderfully good news: it's certainly the highest compliment I could pay anyone. Like it or lump it, display the label or try to scrape it off, you are a mystic yourself from now on. A fully qualified mystic, at that. A seer in your own right, for the rest of your natural life. Take this as a certificate of your proficiency. You will never recover from this sighting of What You Really Are, never quite live it down — I swear to you. You've had it, chum! You have it still.

Why so? For a whole bunch of reasons. Not, of course, because you have no mystical life to live and no mystical work to do. Not because you will (or can) see into your true Nature steadily, without recurring reservations and doubts and endless diversions and interruptions. But because you can now see into it *at will*. AT WILL! How can you be so sure of this? Why because you know exactly *where* to look for it: namely at the spot you call Here. And because you know exactly *when* to look for it: namely at the moment you call Now. And because you know exactly *how* to look for it: namely, the way you look for a dropped coin — by just looking, not by brooding on it and indulging in thoughts and feelings about it. AND because you know exactly *what* it is you're looking for and checking up on: namely, the absence, in the place indicated, of everything (repeat *everything*) you had imagined there. And because you have always to hand the best of tools for the job: namely, that in-pointing finger. Of all its uses, this is the chief.

So it comes about that it's as a mystic and a seer that you are starting to explore with me the mystic vision and the mystic way of life. Without this initiation, *and your active part in it*, the book would turn out to be incomprehensible, or else the case-history of an OAP who really is weak up top and approaching senile dementia...

"Now what's all this?" I hear someone saying, sotto voce. You have followed me so far and got the point. Well, got the general idea. And therefore have dispensed with the physical act of pointing. Unnecessary, in your case. Suitable, perhaps, for the mystically retarded and the mentally handicapped, but for you a silly game which you aren't going to play...

Have I heard correctly?

Alright, be like that! Only let me tell you that, unless you do this simple thing for me and yourself right now, your buying this book was a waste of housekeeping money, and your carting it home was a waste of energy and shopping-bag room, and your further reading of it is going to be an irritating waste of time. Time far better spent curled up with some good mystical cookbook, thumbing through its mouth-watering pictures of mystical dishes from soup to nuts — and keeping well clear of the kitchen with its heat and hassle, and the nursery with its boring games. You are serious about mysticism, and refuse to play silly-buggers with anyone!

Don't kid yourself! You won't get the point until you point, thus turning the arrow of your attention round 180° precisely, and ceasing to overlook the Looker. I assure you that upon this quickest and cheapest and most repeatable and decisive of experiments rests your felicity for evermore. You are at once the laboratory and the apparatus and the researcher and his material and his super-Nobel-Prize-winning discovery. In this pointing lies the whole Point of your existence. In this turning towards the Place you are coming from anyway, to the Hub your life is revolving round anyway, is to be found a hidden blessing and refuge and resource which will never let you down.

No: I'm not asking you to believe a word of all this, still less to understand a thing about it, but just in all simplicity to do what I ask and take what you get. Take it seriously. And stay with it and me until we've worked out this thing together...

Come on! What are you waiting for? Nobody's looking... Thank you!

Hi — just ten seconds are plenty! Much more, and you've started thinking, thinking, thinking about what you see...

And congratulations! Welcome to the club. Not the Junior Seers, but the United Seers.

Now this book is, in essence, your...

3. Autobiography...

no less than mine.

In its peculiar details, of course, in its accidents and non-essentials, your life-story has to be very, very different from my life-story. (And thank the Lord for all his mercies, you may well find yourself saying.) And so, of course, it will be up to you to relate and translate from one to the other, as needed. Also up to you (who surely are in no danger of making the fatal mistake of imitation) to skate lightly over the surface of my story where it's irrelevant to yours.

Why, in that case, does it have to be an autobiography at all? Why not a well-researched and comprehensive survey of the world's most celebrated seers? Or another version of that mystical cookbook, full of exotic recipes for trying out one day, in this life or lives to come? How come this account of the varieties of mystical experience takes so personal a form, is so confined to and so complicated by the history — often bizarre, usually biased, always limited — of one Douglas Edison Harding, to the exclusion of the rest?

No: the reason isn't vanity on his part, but necessity. It's because real mysticism can't stomach desiccated and blood-less abstractions and wind-inflated generalities. Because it is invariably *incarnate*. Because that's how it comes to you and me — like the *individual* fruit pies and *personalised* sweaters we buy in shops — if it comes at all. Because it is in this hardened or hardinged shape that the otherwise inchoate goo called mystical experience is served up to me. To be digestible, to nourish me, it has to be mine and just like this, or it's not even junk food. It's a case of this particular meal, or starvation. But why should I complain?

What — for God's sake — is wrong with this offering I find on my plate — oven fresh and piping hot and well garnished and seasoned to taste? With far more than 57 varieties of sauces. And what a generous helping! Not one of the curious flavours, the pungent smells, the textures slithering and playing around on the tongue, the colours subtly blended, can be spared from the mystical feast which my own life lays before me — if only I have enough lust of life in me, a keen enough appetite for this life which is unique in the history of the universe. A-la-carte and table d'hote meals just aren't served in the mystical bistro. Every dish is to order. Every mouthful unrepeatable.

And all of it arriving by express lift from the same infinitely mysterious kitchen. Mysterious yes, inaccessible no. You and I have just been there. And can go back any time, thanks to the forefinger which is our master key. The oftener the better.

So this new book, like my other books on the same subject,

sprinkled over the years, has to be autobiographical. There's an important difference, however. They were so only to the degree that, otherwise, they would have made no sense at all, or else been quite fraudulent, guidebooks to a country the author had never been anywhere near. This one is deliberately first-personal throughout. They were autobiographical, this is autobiography. Let me tell you why, more precisely.

There are three reasons. Here they are, in order of increasing importance:

(1) I feel a need to piece together the jigsaw puzzle of my eight decades — the bright and beautiful and creditable bits, and the dark and dreary and disgraceful bits, and all those neutral bits in between — till the overall pattern leaps out at me. Undoubtedly it lurks there, poised to spring. In fact, and whatever his or her age the mystic's life emerges as a strictly indivisible design, an organic whole that is very much more than the sum of its parts. One comes to see it, with immense thankfulness, as the Rembrandt portrait it is — those brilliant and complex but rare highlights, surrounded by those great expanses of dun and almost featureless shadow, all combining in a masterpiece. The picture of an ugly old man or woman perhaps, but a beautiful masterpiece all the same, and sombre no more.

(2) My second reason isn't, like the first, the need to put myself in touch with myself, but with others. With you, reader dear, somehow getting across to you exactly what it is we share anyway, and which I perceive as of supreme value to us both. I suspect that some of my failure to communicate in the past has arisen from the habit of putting my case provocatively, in

a way that can irritate and invite misunderstanding.

Less rascality and more tact might help. Less of the *enfant terrible* and more of the *enfant cajolant et persuasif*. It's worth a try. The time has come for a change in tactics, for more disarming manoeuvres, for winning opponents over to my side gradually, by easier stages. The message, bald and crude, still has to read: *Here stand I and here I stick. This — God help me! — is what I am.* But loses no time in adding: *And now let's see how I got this way.* Thus my purpose in what follows is to paint in the comparatively low-toned and ordinary and un-disturbing backcloth against which that outrageous figure of the inverted and headless monster takes shape, and is observed to do so more or less inevitably. I invoke, hopefully, the principle that to know all is to forgive all. A competent defence lawyer, pleading mitigation and bringing out the extenuating circumstances, tries to show that his client just had to be the sort of man he is and to do the sort of thing he did. If I'm accused of regularly stealing all the cats' milk in my neighbourhood, it helps my case to mention that all the cats are grossly overweight and I am skeletal. And, if it should subsequently leak out that, in fact, they are quite willowy, it may help the sympathetic understanding of my case to explain that — appearances notwithstanding – I happen to be the biggest tomcat in town. Similarly, it's a good idea, if you're delivered to the hospital abbreviated by a foot or two, to let the doctor into the secret of what actually happened. By the same token, this book is my detailed account of the very peculiar condition I find myself in (to be shortened by a head is plainly a far more serious thing than by any number of limbs), and of exactly how I came to be like that. Of what hit me, and how, and when, and where, and what it felt like, and so on. And my plan in writing it is to get many more people to check whether they, too, have been topped and truncated. I'm thinking specially of the millions who, understandably, prefer books about people to books about ideas.

(3) My last reason for the autobiographical form this essay takes is easily the most important one. I'm offering a species of psychoanalysis. A rare species certainly (if not an endangered one), but resembling the rest inasmuch as it attributes our grown-up troubles to the *repression* of experience laid down in infancy and early childhood, and sees their cure as the lifting of this repression. Now the repressed material I'm concerned with here isn't Freudian, or Jungian, or Adlerian, and so on. It's more general than that. It's not just an episode or string of episodes in early childhood, or even the overall life-pattern of some deprived or extraordinary child, that's repressed. On the contrary, it's the whole life-style, the inside story and very self of Everychild — a story which contradicts in all respects the story he's required to tell himself later as Everyman — which is thrust down below the conscious level. I won't anticipate here by going into the details of it. In general, let me say that this pristine child — this original self with its inside story — remains intact, alive and kicking harder all the time. It isn't outgrown at all, but grown over. Or rather, ceremonially wept over and coffined and covered with many layers of soil, and held down with many tons of funerary stonework. And of course the incarcerated infant, who doesn't like being buried alive a little bit, gives his adult jailor every kind of hell. More tons of monumental masonry, inscribed with more beautifully nostalgic poetry about our lost childhood and its happy innocence, only make things

worse. No: there's no laying *this* ghost. No shackling this very un-ghostly and substantial and obstreperous infant that might be straight out of Edgar Allan Poe. There's nothing for it but disinterment. I shall get the sum of my life right only by going back to the place where it went wrong. Nowadays there's much talk of rebirthing. Well, my programme here is *re-infanting*. Not so much letting the imprisoned infant up into the full light of adulthood as discovering that in fact he's already right there, and that he is and always will be the light of my Light and the life of my Life. Not so much re-centring on that original Light and Life as noticing that I never came off it for a moment, except in imagination, that I *am* it willy-nilly. And can see it, with perfect clarity, *at will*, once I dare look here.

What this essential infanting comes to, in non-verbal and real-life terms, we have seen in our Pointing experiment. What it comes to in detailed working out and day-by-day practice, we shall see in the following chapters. What it requires now and always is that we should cease this disastrous repression, and be *consciously* as transparent and wide open as we were in the cradle, and in fact have never left off being. As busted wide open. As naive, if you like.

In a word, be *suckers*?

Not quite. As we have already noticed in passing, it's the thoroughly grown-up grown-up who is so naïve — naïve in the bad sense of being gullible. So unquestioningly does he trim himself and his world to fit the social templates that he's scarcely aware of their existence. The true infant, on the other hand, is naïve in the good sense of being artless and simple, and as yet trimmed to no templates. And the true mystic, infanting, is naïve in this good sense, too. So that you could say that he is something...

4. ...of a Simpleton

I conclude this Introduction with a just-so story — the story of how this literary creature of mine got its tail. And, more particularly, how its author got the appendage of *simpleton*. In a round-about way I came by it, I think, in Bloomington, Indiana — a city where, way back in '72, I talked a group of people into pointing in at you-know-what.

It's not the sort of soubriquet that I would naturally, and without encouragement from outside, have bestowed on myself. It's not my first choice of a flag of convenience to sail under. No: I have to thank Professor Douglas H. Hofstadter of Indiana University (who could have been, I suppose, a member of that group) for the inspiration. I said thank, and I mean thank.

About a book of mine entitled *On Having No Head* — in matter much the same as this book, in manner very different — he writes:

> "We have here been presented with a charmingly child-ish and solipsistic view of the human condition. It is something that, at an intellectual level, offends and appals us: can anyone seriously entertain such matters without embarrassment?"

'Childish', mark you. Not childlike. 'Embarrassing' and 'offensive', like the village idiot that the village wants to see committed to institutional care, because he thinks he's a teapot, and behaves accordingly all over the place. 'Appall-ing', too. Later on, he comes up with the word 'nutty'. The Professor, with admirable directness, surely doesn't mince his words.

All the same, he does bring himself to devote some ten pages of his and (Professor Daniel C. Dennett's) collection entitled '*The Mind's I*' to excerpts from my book and comments on them. Well, I'm grateful for that, too. When one has a product to sell (and I do, I do), any exposure in the human superstore is better than no exposure at all. Accordingly, I'm not complaining that my goods are displayed in the baby-care section, along with dummies and nappies (pacifiers and diapers to you, Professor), and lead-free building blocks in primary colours. After all, I asked for it. I guess this sort of thing goes along with *infanting*, is a part of the package. So be it.

For the record, I have to add that Hofstadter, warming up towards the end of his commentary, does generously concede:

"Only a powerful vision such as Harding's Himalayan experience can return us to that primordial sense of self and otherness which is at the root of the problems of consciousness, soul, and self."

The way I read him, Hofstadter is saying something like this:

Yes: the babe within does have a vital message for me. The snag is that it comes out in baby talk. Yes: he does have a vision. The snag is that it is the vision of a simpleton, of an endearing but infinitely gullible little visionary. Fortunately, however, I don't have to take on the messenger with the message. To learn from him I don't have to wear a nappy and suck a dummy and become a sucker, any more than to learn from audiotapes and videotapes I have to become a tapeworm.

The rest of this book can be taken as my detailed reply,

more in terms of a life lived than an apologia worked out, of this interpretation of Hofstadter. Meanwhile here, in the tiniest of nutshells, is the kernel of that reply. It takes the form of two sets of questions:

First, about gullibility. Which (I repeat) is the gullible one, the sucker? Is it the out-dwelling grown-up who (hypnotised by language and the desperate need to belong at all costs) hallucinates an inedible and decaying meatball plumb in the centre of his universe, and proceeds to live from and — oh yes! — to die from that monstrosity? Or is it the indwelling infant who (whatever his chronological age) is impervious to the Great Hypnotists's passes and ploys, and so lives from the primordial Emptiness at the mid-point of his universe — an emptiness that is chock-full of that universe? In brief, is it the shit-head or the no-head? It has to be one or the other. That's the brutal truth.

Second, about health — about sanity and wholeness and genuineness. Which is the healthy one? Is it the un-mystical grown-up, whose thinking is telling him one story and whose feeling — his native instincts — are telling him an altogether different story, and who senses no need and sees no chance of working at them until they come together in one story: a story that's as intellectually sound as it is emotionally satisfying? Or is it the mystical grown-up, who commits himself to and succeeds in that formidable — but infinitely rewarding — task of integration?

Yes, I admit it, dear reader. These are leading questions, short on neutrality, long on rhetoric... and, I'm pretty sure, unfair to Hofstadter.

However, they will do very well for leading us into the Autobiography of this highly complex Simpleton.

2. THE CHILD I WAS

1. The Simpleton and the Complexiton

Looking through the previous chapter after a few days' interval, I'm startled to find how gastronomical it turned out to be. Almost as if this ex-officer from East Anglia had, malgré lui, been channelling that other officer — of similar countenance but superior rank and fame and fortune — from Kentucky, with his finger lickin' and lip smackin'. But there's a serious point I want to slip in here. It is that the link between mysticism and asceticism is more cultural than essential. Ramana Maharshi — one of the greatest of modern mystics — is said to have had a hearty appetite, and he was fairly bulbous from middle age. Potei, the popular Chinese-Japanese bodhisattva (a Buddha in the making) is represented as near-globular. For myself, I'm happy to say that I enjoy my food immensely. If I weren't so unchoosy, you might call me a gourmet. My story is that eating, when given enough attention, can be one of the many varieties of mystical experience — one that has the advantage of being regularly laid on, at that. A story not unconnected, I grant you, with the fact that nowadays, whereas I will pass muster in front elevation, in side elevation I'm moderately conference-pear shaped. At a more superficial and personal level, the explanation of this epicurean tendency could be that I'm still reacting to my mother's stern pronouncement that one eats to live, and for no other reason. Incidentally and at the same level, I suspect that much of my adult life — not least the mystical aspect of it — could be read as a protracted rebellion against maternal injunctions and prohibitions. In which case, how grateful I am for them!

As for this book itself and the writing of it, I think it will prove — in contrast to its subject matter — to be no piece of cake at all. I can already see that it's going to be much more of a challenge than I had anticipated. And, please God, much more of an opportunity, too. The plain fact is that I shall not only be breaking old rules, but breaking new ground in the art of autobiography. Nothing like it has been attempted before. Who knows what treasures my plowshare may unearth? Or where it will get stuck?

Much of the challenge stems from the fact that I'm not telling the story of just one personality but two, two masquerading under one name. Conceivably it would help if, splitting the book down the middle, I were to dispose of one of them before taking on the other. But that wouldn't work. If I'm to do justice to the fact that these two characters carry on simultaneously in parallel, I shall have to bring them together repeatedly, pointing out their total interdependence no less than their total difference. I have christened them the Simpleton and the Complexiton — a sharp and crucial distinction which nevertheless scarcely begins to indicate how very disparate they are. For it's not that, as in the case of Dr. Jekyll and Mr. Hyde, they are profoundly contrasting members of the same species, but that they belong to different species, to altogether different orders of being. Pick, blindfold, any two from a checklist of the world's fauna and flora and you will never get a pair as ill-assorted as the couple which make up the subject of this autobiography. As ill-assorted: yet, paradoxically, as well-assorted, in the sense that they are perfectly matched. I'm reminded of the fungus and the alga that, setting up business together on (for example) my grandfather's tombstone, trade under the single name *lichen.* Prior to 1866, lichen was thought to be one plant. In much the same way, prior to 1942, I thought myself to be one person: since when I have been noticing, with growing astonishment, how wrong I was. But again, the lichen analogy is quite inadequate. After all, fungi and algae are both subjects of the Animal Kingdom, whereas the Simpleton and the Complexiton belong to different kingdoms, realms that have precisely Nothing in common.

My difficulties are compounded by the fact that, blind to my dual nature, the world insists on addressing me as plain Douglas Harding and not the Douglas Harding Partnership or Douglas Harding & Co., and has trained me to respond with a plain 'I' having no tendency to develop into a royal 'we'. All conspiring to deny what I am. And to perpetuate the Great Lie that I am what I look like: that what 'I' am for you and what 'I' am for myself are two views of the selfsame thing, related as the inside of this book is to its cover. A lie and an absurdity I had yet to learn when, just starting to talk, I said: 'Baby want teddy,' or 'Douglas coughing coughing,' and the trickster word 'I' (which should carry an official Anglo-American health warning) didn't figure in my vocabulary at all.

But now, stuck with the word, at least let me try to use it intelligently here, in the interests of self-knowledge instead of self-deception. In particular, my aim is to be clear about which I is holding the floor at any one time. Is it I the Simpleton who's speaking, or I the Complexiton? I(S) or I(C)? And in this way to frustrate their knavish trick of imperceptibly merging and switching identities, and making out that they are one and the same storyteller telling one and the same story about one and the same person.

In this chapter it is I(C)'s turn, and in the following chapter it will be I(S)'s turn, to give an account of my early childhood. This done, it will be perfectly plain just how I(C) turns I(S) up-side down, and exactly what this means in real-life terms.

But don't get me wrong here. I'm not looking at this double life of mine with a view to correcting it, but to waking up to what's actually going on. The most needful and searching and comprehensive therapy is the discovery that one doesn't need therapy at all, thank you very much, but is fine as one is. Simpleton and Complexiton can, and should, and actually do, live comfortably together. It's self-deception — the pretense that the Simpleton is dead and buried so deep that he can never give trouble, much less stage a come-back, that plagues our race. This is the disease that starts attacking all humans very early in life, and nearly always gets worse and worse till death: though some fortunate ones called mystics or seers do — for whatever reason and no credit to them — grow out of it. Or rather, snap out of it.

The main sign of this endemic disease is unremitting and many-facetted *hallucination*. Which is unhealthy and debilitating, as well as exceedingly unpractical — when you don't know what the blazes you are up to. When you do know, when you 'hallucinate' consciously and by design and within limits, why then it's hallucination no longer. It's... Well, before the end of the chapter we shall see exactly what it is.

Meanwhile, may I make a suggestion? It is that, as you now go on to read the first version of my early life — which is as truthful as I(C) know how to make it — you keep your eyes skinned for instances of the hallucination I speak of. I assure you that (as will be revealed by the Simpleton in his version) they are there all over the place, more plentiful than nuts in autumn, and twice as nutty.

2. 107 High Street, Lowestoft

The French, with more accuracy than politesse, are inclined to describe the British as a nation of shopkeepers. In that case, I'm truly British.

My father had a smallish fruit, flowers, and vegetable business in Lowestoft, a smallish seaside town at the eastern extremity of England, where it sticks out a bare and well-rounded backside at Europe. Not unfitting to talk of my birthplace thus, discharging as it did (and maybe still does) large volumes of untreated sewage daily into the North Sea, for tidal distribution along its beaches. It's a windswept, grey, and mostly High-Victorian borough uncertain whether its business is netting fish or summer visitors. My maternal grandfather, Grandpa Garrard — a gruff little man, producer of twelve aunts and uncles — was the butcher at Alderton, a village some thirty miles to the south. And my paternal grandfather, whom I adored, was the manager of a posh family grocer's in Colchester — a town with delightful Roman and Civil War connections — still further south.

Sometimes I think it's in the blood (a Thatcherite or corner-shop gene?), and that I, too, am a shopkeeper, spry and poised and customer-oriented as a Venus Fly Trap is fly-oriented: dressing my window, and polishing and stacking my wares with the best merchandise to the front, all drastically marked down to pull in the customers. (Welcome to you, dear reader!) This I do know: one of my favourite early games was Shop, in which I offered a comprehensive choice of acorns, pine cones, half-grown windfalls, plum stones, whelk and cockle shells, unidentified objects, and odd buttons — at bargain prices. What more could anyone want? Lots of wonderful things to sell, never quite so many customers as one would like. Do we ever outgrow these early patterns?

I was born on February 12th, 1909, in the front bedroom over the shop at 107, High Street, just behind the fascia which read:

FRUITERER E.C. HARDING FLORIST

executed in curly-serifed and beautifully shaded signwriting. Freda followed around a year later, Geoffrey a year later than that. Stop.

I see myself as a round-faced child, with red cheeks and very black hair, and the strong podgy hands of a good brick-layer — or hoister of 1-cwt. sacks of potatoes. Very talkative (when given half a chance), inquisitive, imaginative, given to scowling sulks when thwarted or humiliated. Just like my mother, prone to self-pity: 'martyr' she called me, and in lots of little ways made sure I lived up to the title. Literal minded, trusting, easily hurt, proud, I was distressed at the merry laughter of the maid when I rushed to get salt to put on the tail of the mouse that had just scrabble-skated across the polished living-room lino. And at the same laughter when, having been assured that the rabbit I'd just observed strolling down the High Street was Imagination, I most seriously asked whether Imagination had a white tail. Oh yes, I fancied myself and I hated ridicule, hated being put down. In the eyes of people who didn't like what I was up to, I was a remarkably conceited and obsessional child: in the eyes of those who did, I was a remarkably self-assured and one-pointed and persistent child. Take your pick. What interested me took over, to the exclusion of all else. I went crazy about it. I had it for breakfast and dinner and high tea! High tea with fruit that was just about to go off. A few crazes lasted (some have never left me, for instance a passion for coloured lights): others duly fizzled out. All my life I've been incapable of doing things by halves. It's a case of all, or next-door-to-nothing, with this brother. Don't trust him to keep several pots on the boil at once.

The house-cum-shop had everything, everything that such a child could desire. Best of all, a view. Mounted at the top of what had been a cliff, its rear windows took in a rectangle of North Sea. Ah, that deep perilous sea, with all its secrets and moodiness! Its occasional carpet of flashing light, rolled out from the sun rising over the horizon all the way up to — why to Prince Douglas, of course. Its terrible dangers. I watched a coaster tilt violently and go down — hit, they said, by a torpedo from a German submarine. I saw a drifter being driven ashore and smashed in a storm. I saw a line of German warships, silhouetted against the dawn horizon, as they shelled the town — shelled us — while Father prayed to the Lord for his protection. (On principle, he had turned down the offer of shelter next door, in the cinema's strong cellar.) And I'll never forget the day — it was in 1914 — when that fleet of little Belgian fishing boats, dangerously loaded down with women and children fleeing from the Kaiser's armies, sailed past. Yes: unbelievably hemmed in though my childhood was, it mercifully opened out eastwards onto the Wild, the Beyond, fascinating, boundless, infinitely more promising than threatening. That eastern sea has never ceased to flood my veins.

From the outlook to the look-out — to the house with a view — was a narrowing and a come-down, all right. There was the shop — shopworn and tatty but tidy, low-ceilinged

and a nasty old step down from the street — about which
more later. At the back of the shop a poky kitchen, with its
steaming hiss and clatter and succession of promising smells,
its slightly sinister beetle-black range, and brown stoneware
sink that felt like wet sandpaper. And, at its rear, the so-called
living room, alive with little of its own except the view. Over
the shop, a couple of not-too-pleasant bedrooms, each with its
complement of marble-topped wash-stand, ewer and basin,
its brass-knobbly bedstead with chamber (our contraction of
chamber-pot) peeping from beneath its counterpane skirt:
the whole packaged between four walls and floor relentlessly
covered to the last inch with the sort of mock-floral patterns
there ought to be a bylaw against, patterns of some world or
other — if not *the* world. And over these the whitewashed
attics where we children slept and dreamed. Very plain and
bare, but opening out onto a minor glory. If you happened
to wake up at night, there — so close you might almost lean
out and touch it — was one of the street arc lights, blazing
shivery blue-white, quietly muttering and spluttering to itself.
A delight extinguished, alas in 1915 was it?, on account of
the wicked Kaiser's Zeppelins and Taubes.

I suppose that every home has its bad places, just as every
homeland has its bad lands. The badness of No. 107 was
concentrated in the basement, the cellar, as we called it. Pitch
dark for the most part, murky and musty all over, it was used
for storing junk and sacks of potatoes. Also it was the home
of rats who (in contrast to us children as Mother would have
us) were heard and not seen. It owed some of its importance
and all its inescapability to the House of Commons (Lav was
slightly rude, W.C. disgusting, Shithouse the Sin against the
Holy Ghost) with its interesting and peculiar funnel set in a

deck scrubbed till the grain stood out like a ploughed field, and a pile of torn-up newspapers that had a vicious habit of running out when most needed. Ammunition, we called it. (There was the bathroom, only a hip bath lugged into the living room on Friday evenings. An arrangement that had much to recommend it, specially when the fire was blazing and Dorothy the maid crooned to us as she scrubbed our backs. Darling Dorothy!) Also here in the basement — no words will do justice to its menace — was the Coal Hole, inhabited by a goblin with piercing eyes set in a tight-skinned and black-boot-polished head. He was the horror who sometimes escaped from his hole and pursued me in nightmares: nightmares that went on and on after I'd been woken up and led round the bedroom by my worried parents, so that I could see for myself that he'd gone away. And, in a corner near his Hole, was the copper; and, once a week, crouched over it, a hairy and warty old washerwoman who might have been a second cousin of the goblin, and probably boiled and ate small boys between meals. All in all, the cold-cellar-basement of No. 107 High Street was a tremendous place. The never-far-off dark night of this young soul: yet, like the less localised dark nights that were to follow in later years, by no means all miserable and goblin-infested. Without it, the delicious morning light, the light of that eastern sea which it had no view of at all, could never have shone. Not on your sweet life. Nor, without its support, could those living quarters and that shop have been held aloft in the warm and kindly sunlight.

The shop was a special joy. A scene of bustle and clatter, of freshness and exquisite colours and smells, with its flow of assorted customers ranging from hoity-toity to what my mother called *common*, her tone of voice hinting at unplumbed depths of grubbiness and delinquency. Also there were friendly and jokey growers of fruit and vegetables; and, on slack afternoons, the odd commercial traveller, garrulous and ingratiating, and getting round Father so easily with their pious chit-chat. With me still are the divine scent of mimosa and eggs-and-bacon (our name for those small narcissi with yellow centres), purple-black grapes with their dusty bloom nestling in crisp blue tissue paper, the happy clanging of the till as it rang up yet another tuppence ingested, and those spiked metal shields marked FANCY and CHOICE and EXTRA CHOICE, and 1d, 2d, 3d, and even 4d a pound for the choicest fruit. (Spotty apples — spots for short — a euphemism for quarter-bad-ones, went to poor and often barefoot children for a farthing or a ha'penny a pound.)... That shop, with all the wonderful people and goods that came into and went out of it, wasn't just our little world. It was our inter-face with the great world, the world of inconceivably rich and inconceivably poor, of plorable gentlefolk and middle-folk (which in a vague way but with absolute determination we belonged to) and deplorable un-gentlefolk, of war and the peace that was and was to come, of nation and king and far-flung empire, of exotic lands — ruled by monkeys for all we knew — which our bananas and brazil nuts and so on came from, astounding probabilities and possibilities...

It was our interface with the world to which we did *not* belong. Oh no! For we were different. We were *un*worldly! We were the Lord's people, in the world but not of the world.

By the Lord's mysterious design, our immediate neighbours could not have been more *this*-worldly and incongruous, more calculated to bring out just how different we were. A small nut — nutty enough in the eyes of the many townspeople, but impossible to crack — we found ourselves squeezed between a pair of formidable nutcrackers. On the north a flea-pit picture palace called the Cosy Corner, and on the south a very uncosy pub — a roaring pub on Saturday nights — called the Spreadeagle. Such was my upbringing that I saw the posters outside the Cosy Corner as invitations to unspeakable orgies, and heard the noises that issued from within, and from the bowels rather than the mouth of the Spreadeagle, as the muted clamour of Hell. Not always, I confess, an altogether disagreeable clamour. That wicked thumping honky-tonk-ish stuff was apt to send my feet tapping and my blood racing, and to sound almost heavenly in my music-starved ears. And, by Heaven, it still does! Perhaps more than ever. So many of the mystical peaks of my life have been set against a background of music with the irresistible beat of a Caribbean steel-drum band's rendering of Edith Piaff's *Milord*. Unseemly, if you go by so much of that nice, respectable mystical literature. But what the hell? Folks who suppose that God is a high-class God, seemly or decent or sensible, aren't living in his world at all. No-one is so vulgar, so unholy! Even at that very young age the foundations were being laid of my suspicion — followed by my certainty — that Heaven is at least as much a Cosy Corner and a Spreadeagle as it is those holier premises belonging to Edgar Charles Harding, family fruiterer and florist and potato merchant — and Exclusive Plymouth Brother.

3. Beloved Brethren

The Plymouth Brethren are a fundamentalist sect founded early in the 19th century by one John Nelson Darby, a scholarly and desperately hard-working and somewhat dotty Anglican priest who decided he wasn't so special after all.

His Holy Bible told him that every true Christian man is a
priest in the eyes of God, ordained not by Pope or bishop but
by the Spirit to teach and preach and to conduct the service
of the bread and the wine at the Lord's table. Only men, only
the Brothers are called to priesthood. Plymouth Sisters sit
silent in Meeting, soberly be-hatted and long-skirted and
long-faced and prim-lipped, following the injunctions of that
prince of chauvinists, Saint Paul. It's true that, as to doctrine,
the Brethren differ little from the great mass of evangelical
fundamentalist Christians: on the principle of justification
by faith and not works they accept Jesus Christ as their personal Saviour, and his death on the cross as the terrible price
paid for the forgiveness of their sins and their admission to
eternal bliss. Nor are they more given to bible-thumping, or
to fantastic interpretations of scripture, than the others are.
No: it's their translation of the texts — particularly those
insisting on the believer's separation from an unbelieving
world — into actual behaviour that they are exceptional.
Their inflexible rule is: 'Come out from among them and be
ye separate,' saith the Lord, 'and keep ye up the habit, go ye
on separating from the separated ones — the insufficiently
separated ones — if ye are to remain My People.' Ever since
their foundation, the Brethren have been splitting up, each
schism a traumatic division into a more and a less exclusive
and puritanical faction, notable for the bitter refusal of the
former to have anything more to do with the latter. The end
product of this long process of fission and self-righteous
withdrawal (a favourite term of theirs) was the aptly-named
Exclusive Brethren, as distinct from the Open Brethren, the
Kelley Brethren, the Glanton Brethren, and other deplorably
lax bodies.

Of this sect, my parents were utterly devoted members, steeped in exclusiveness. So were all my near relations on my father's side.

Mother was a convert to the Plymouth Brethren, and therefore did have some knowledge of church-and-chapel Christianity of the evangelical kind — knowledge which, I fear, only made her more intolerant. Father was a PB by birthright. His parents joined the Brethren long before he and my Aunt Mabel were born. We three children, accordingly, were third generation PBs. (My sister Freda's children and grandchildren are fourth and fifth generation PBs — a solemn thought!) The cumulative power over us of this ancestral apartheid is hard to overestimate. Built into us was the conviction that we were absolutely right and all the others were absolutely wrong, that we the Exclusives were the Chosen Ones, and that the rest of so-called Christians — including an unspecified number of withdrawn-from sects of Plymouth Brethren — were certainly unchosen, and probably hellbound. Not that we called ourselves the Exclusives. Oh dear no! We were the Little Flock, the Meeting, the Brethren, the Lord's People, the Saints gathered in Lowestoft (saints forsooth! In Lowestoft, if you please!), or whatever. And, by an unspoken logic not lost on me, we constituted the central concern and ultimate raison d'être of the Universe, ranging from stars to fish scales. The littleness of the Little Flock (often down to a dozen, or even half a dozen, locally, and some of them — according to Mother — rather too 'common' for us to be really intimate with) did nothing to unsettle this conviction. Understandably, God was particular about the company he kept throughout eternity. Looking round the rougher parts of town, and speculating about the goings-on

of our immediate neighbours, I could see he had a point.
Looking round the dear Brothers and Sisters in the Meeting, I saw that point less clearly. Well, God is kind — to his
own — and puts up with a good deal of 'commonness'. And
at least we were doing what he told us to do. We were being
separate, as separate as we knew how. And then some. For a
start, the only newspapers we took were old ones, strictly for
wrapping potatoes in, and — with a fine appropriate gesture
— for wiping our bottoms with. So far as I can recollect, the
literature that found its way into our house, besides the Bible
and the Brethren's voluminous commentaries thereon, was
restricted to a few the-cat-is-on-the-mat items for tiny tots
(after all, we had to learn to read), *Pilgrim's Progress, Pears
Encyclopaedia*, a work with the promising title *Enquire Within
Upon Everything*, a dictionary of sorts, a so-called Doctor's
Book much consulted by my mother; and, of course, later on,
a minimum of school-books for homework. However I did,
from the age of about twelve, manage to smuggle in several
Dickens' novels under this school-book head: which I found
it prudent to read (along with even more worldly literature
such as the *The Adventures of Sherlock Holmes*) locked in the
W.C. When I was twenty — no less! — my father discovered
a small cache of books on pop psychology which I'd picked
up secondhand, and ceremonially burned them. No great
loss, of course. But the fact which still astonishes me is that
I scarcely protested at all. Thus firmly was I held under the
Brethren's thumb, even then.

'Friendship with the world is enmity with God,' was the
favourite stick to beat us children with, whenever we showed
signs of getting at all pally with our school-fellows. They
weren't allowed into our home, and we were forbidden to

enter theirs — a rule I rarely managed to break. Since, most of the time, we were the only Exclusive children in the town, and since the grown-up Exclusives we consorted with were notably un-playful and solemn, we were forced to amuse ourselves — without letting on we were having fun. Overt laughter, any playful remark, was likely to bring down the awful warning "God will require you to account for every idle word". Maternal warning it was — are converts to a faith ever as relaxed about it as birthright members? Father was less austere: he actually had about three permitted jokes — semi-holy ones about Scotch Brethren, and how well we got to know them! — and his smile was never for long repressed. But I was a crafty lad. I remember one Sunday afternoon, when even to look for sea shells along the shore was having fun and contrary to God's holy will, I explained to Mother that I was finding out how clever their Designer was. And I got away with it. She got a lovely story to intimidate her fellow Plymouth Sisters with, about her pious little boy — ha, ha! And I got my shells. We both won.

Fortunately this doctrine of apartheid couldn't be applied to official school hours. All it could do was to ban extracurricular activities, including prize-givings and non-compulsory games and school excursions. Unwisely, I once allowed myself to be cast as a minor character in *Twelfth Night*. I can still feel the public humiliation when my mother, having found me out — *after* my splendid costume had been made to measure — forced me to refuse to have anything whatever to do with the play. And yet — though I was terribly ashamed — it didn't strike me as unfair that I should carry the can for my parents' eccentricities. However reluctantly, I was a dyed-in-the-wool little PB at heart. Thanks to school, a decreasingly Exclusive one, but a PB all the same.

During the War, most of the Exclusives were 'conscientious objectors' or 'conshies'. Of these, some were drafted into the NCC or Non-combatant Corps — that most execrated branch of the Army. Others, including my uncle Earnest Yaxley, refused to wear any sort of uniform. He was jailed in Wormwood Scrubs — a penal establishment of scarcely imaginable severity to my young mind, including floor-scrubbing day and night, interrupted only for meals of the bitterest and most horribly worm-infested wormwood. Actually he had a hard time all right — and made damn sure he did. Father was luckier, and less set on martyrdom. He appeared before various local tribunals, appealing against military service on religious grounds, and eventually was excused because his heart was somewhat dicky, and because he was (with doubtful consistency) a contractor to the Navy, supplying large quantities of potatoes and so forth to the monitor anchored for the duration in the harbour. Nevertheless we children weren't allowed, years after 1918, to forget that Father was no credit to the community: in the eyes of many a coward, and a profiteering coward, at that. I have a vivid recollection of walking to the docks with him, dogged by a sinister character shouting abuse. Who knows? — his son might have been killed in Flanders. (In fact, though there was something in the profiteering jibe, Father would rather have gone to the lions than deny his Lord. I've known no braver man.) I shared his pain, and loved him so much. I felt implicated: as if I, too, in my loyalty to that realm 'above the bright blue sky', had been obliged to betray my earthly country.

But I was no humourless and hard-done-by kid. Cheerfulness kept breaking in, and there were many compensations.

Not a few of them arising, I'm happy to say, from the daily
and weekly religious life of the Brethren.

We were not allowed to forget the dear Lord for long.
Before every meal, Father came out with an extemporary but
predictable grace: a thank you, O Lord, for all your mercies.
It was spontaneous inasmuch as it emerged with great hes-
itation and difficulty, as if a search were on for exactly the
right turn of phrase; and it was predictable inasmuch as the
search always arrived at the same place as last time. I found
a certain excitement — the mild tension of a punter who
has backed a sure winner — in waiting for the inevitable
outcome. Then there were morning and evening prayers —
equally spontaneous and almost equally predictable. First,
Father read a lengthy passage from the Bible, then we all
(including the maid, who wasn't 'in the Meeting') flopped to
our knees while Father addressed Gord. (This isn't a misprint.
The Exclusives worship a deity of this name, perhaps to rhyme
with Lord, his other title.) There followed blessings upon
various named relatives belonging to the Meeting, gratitude
for the Love that gave itself for us poor sinners, aspirations
to live ever closer to that Love, and renewed undertakings
to keep ourselves unspotted from the world. All in the name
of Jesus Christ our Lord, A-men. Not Ar-men, as in those
very sub-standard school prayers.

Often embarrassing, sometimes excruciatingly funny, sometimes plain excruciating, all this was nevertheless impressive.
Then as now, my father was for me the sincerest and most
loving and loveable man imaginable, wholly guileless, gentleness itself, with a good heart and the smile of a child. Yet a
man strong and real. Moreover, in his own way — along with
not a few other Exclusives — so true a mystic that I guess I

caught the condition from him. The fact that he was also a little man, a deplorably bigoted little man, nervous in manner, rather shamefaced and lip-trembly and tip-toe when holding forth at Meeting, and quite incapable of negotiating the easiest of those tongue-twisters the Old Testament is a minefield of (he was even unsure whether the Whore of Babylon was a Hore or a Wore) — none of this really mattered. Not even when, with a terrible resolve amounting to self-immolation, he elected to read one whole chapter of the Bible to us each day, relentlessly, from *Genesis* 1 to *Revelation* 22 — including not only the indecent bits beloved of us children, but many chapters that read like this:

> And their border was towards Jezreel, and Chesulloth and Shunem. And Hapharaim, and Shiou, and Anaharath. And Rabbith, and Kishion, and Abiz. And Remeth, and En-gannim, and En-haddah, and Bethpazzez. And the coast reaches to Tabor, and Shahzimah, and Beth-shemesh...

And so on and on and on. Which was asking for trouble. Nor was the spiritual message of such readings or splutterings immediately plain to us. Of course, it had to be there (this was God's Holy Word!) and could be counted on — Hapharaim and Shion and Anaharath and all — to set us up for the day. Somehow.

But the focus and mainstay of the Brethren's life was not so much the home as the Meeting. In fact, up to six meetings a week, held in the barest and dreariest of halls smelling of grey-wash and gas and rising damp, with bottom-numbing bentwood chairs arranged round a kitchen-type table covered with green baize. A noisome coke stove, coconut matting, and some moth-eaten hassocks for the Sisters (was it that female legs have something wrong with them, or was it to make up for their owners' having to keep their mouths tightly shut?) — these were the only concessions to comfort. There was, of course, no piano, much less a harmonium or organ. We sang hymns unaccompanied, and the results were often a calamity. A Brother (rarely Father, who knew his way round the pitfalls of the better Flock's hymnbook), having given out a hymn, would start off the singing at the wrong pitch, or to a tune that even he didn't know, or whose metre didn't fit the words at all, and the whole project had to be abandoned — not abruptly, alas, but trailing off into a kind of groan. And even when the projected tune was recognisable, and the pitch negotiable, and the metre fairly close-fitting, our paean of praise to Gord was cacophonous enough — not lustily so, but in the feeblest and most tentative way. One could only hope that Gord, unlike the deity they sang to in those other places, was tone-deaf, too. Or above all that sort of thing.

Sunday morning — correction, Lord's day morning — say the holiest occasion of the week — the Breaking of Bread. A cottage loaf in a basket, and a large tumbler full of port, appeared on the now white-clothed table. Passages from the New Testament story of the Last Supper (J.N. Darby's translation) were read out. Extemporary prayers were prayed, their often tearful sincerity doing much to make up for their stumbling incoherence. The bread was broken and passed round for each Brother and Sister to pluck a morsel out of. Followed by the tumbler of wine, from which each took a sip. We children, of course, along with the rare outsider who had wandered in, were just spectators. There wasn't much to grip our attention. The meeting dragged on for eighty minutes or so, at least sixty of which were spent in silence while we waited — not without some anxiety or even impatience — for the Holy Spirit to move the next speaker, or at least the hands of the clock.

From the age of around four or five I was brought along to the Breaking-of-Bread Meeting, where I was expected to sit through to the end with almost no fidgeting. Not such an impossible demand to be made of a young child as you might imagine. If ever you happen to attend a Sunday-morning Quaker meeting (superficially not unlike a PB one), I think you will be impressed by the quietness of the young children, throughout the fifteen minutes of more-or-less complete silence which — as a rule — is the period of their attendance: after which they are led off to Sunday school. For myself, I owe much to this early training in stillness. The next time one of my sterner Buddhist critics asks me, pointedly, when I put in my stint of sitting meditation, I must remember to reply, casually, 'from the age of four to twenty-one, and up to six sessions a week'. But I would have to admit that I found a way to cheat, to beat the system. Sitting there, just like those grown-ups so prim and so still and with firmly closed eyes, I acquired an undeserved and unsought reputation for piety. In fact I was not — except for a conversion period between seventeen and eighteen — contemplating the sufferings of the Lord and his risen glory, but my latest passion or craze — sea shells, ammonites (the sort I dug out of the cliff, not the Old Testament), butterflies, pressed tree leaves, pressed wild flowers, the meticulous drawing I was making of the buildings opposite, Euclid, my fast-growing collection of new and curious and useful words... And when, at seventeen,

I began my architectural training, I learned to devote every meeting of the week — whether it was for the breaking of bread, or prayer, or reading and discussion — to those studies. Quite easily I fell into a light trance, while there unrolled before me the studies of the past few days, including plans and elevations and sections of the great buildings of all ages and styles, ranging from the Pyramid of Cheops to the Paris Opera. The examination results were so remarkable that I was packed off, at nineteen plus, with a minute grant from Suffolk County Council, to complete my studies at University College, London. I have to add that letting me go there was to prove, from my parents' point of view, the most tragic mistake they ever made. It finally cured me of Brethrenism.

Another undetected benefit — of a very different and more controversial kind — I owed to those meetings. In particular, to the Sunday morning meeting. It was my father's custom, when clearing away afterwards, to pour the unused wine — at least half a large tumbler of that richly coloured and fruity nectar — down the sink. Having secretly sampled the stuff, I thought: What a dreadful waste! So — deceitful child that I was — I volunteered to take over the cleaning-up chore from him, somehow hinting that here was a humble job I wanted to do for the most exalted of motives. Along the lines of the hymn we had sung some years earlier:

> We are but little children weak,
> And not of any high estate:
> What can we do for Jesus' sake,
> Who is so high and good and great?

Well, I could do his washing up. Father was delighted, of

course. Little did he realise that, from the age of about ten, his eldest regularly ambled home from Meeting with inside aglow, through strangely luminous and mobile streets. Thus early and thus agreeably was I initiated into the alcoholic variety of mystical experience. I have found no need or inclination to pursue the matter further.

And, even if Father had tumbled to what was going on, he wouldn't have given me a hard time. Not so, Mother.

4. Mother and Son
Not so, Mother.

You will have gathered that she and I didn't get on at all. Oh what wounds we inflicted on each other! The tortuous and painful track of my early life with her is signalled by five or six landmarks:

The first. I'm no more than three. Either my brother Geoffrey is about to be born or has just been born. Anyway, here am I at the foot of the stairs, howling and stamping and flailing my arms because I'm not allowed to go up and see her. The real reason for my rage, of course, is this intruder into the family, this monster who's usurping her attention and love...

The second landmark, though more prominent, is shaped somewhat like the first. I'm now six. The year is 1915. The War is in its second year. Aunt Margaret and four bumptious cousins are staying with us because her husband, Uncle Earnest Yaxley, preferring prison to putting on a uniform of any sort, has left his family destitute and homeless. Result: our house is disgustingly full. I say as much, and more, to these bouncy cousins, with unveiled indications that the Yaxley lot are intruders, and as such have less right to the limited amenities of the place than the Harding lot have. Tearfully, this appalling rudeness is reported to their mother, who even more tearfully reports the same to my mother. Boiling over with indignation and shame, she commands Father to beat the hell out of me. Or PB words to that effect. Which he, bless his darling heart, can't bring himself to do. So Mother, I guess almost as furious with him as with me, snatches up a cherry-wood walking stick and rushes upstairs and larrups me on the bottom with the thing. I writhe about a good deal on the bed, but the pain goes almost unnoticed. The mental agony (inconceivable, inconceivable that *she* should be doing this to me!) is so sharp that any physical agony is overridden, if not obliterated. Stuck-up, self righteous, amoral kid that I am, I have no sense of guilt whatever, only of outrage. Horribly insulted and humiliated, I spend the rest of the night scrawling messages of black hate and hurt on scraps of paper and distributing them around the bedroom. In the morning, Dorothy, the maid or mother's help, finds them and, duly shocked, takes them to Mother. Pretty soon, everyone knows the whole story. For some days a reserve — as if a sudden death or some unmentionable disease has struck us — descends on the joint families. And that cherry-wood object flaunts itself there in the hallway, shameless among decent umbrellas and things, a filthy monument — not to cruelty and injustice, but to love become loathing, and the general nastiness of existence.

This is the time when I start my Domesday Book, a register in code of Mother's offences against me, bearing the cryptic title MRR — a species of acronym standing for Mother's Rottenness. I'm never to blame, of course: all is vindictiveness on her part, none is delinquency on my part! That beating, however, was the first and the last, though there followed much loose and self-justifying talk of 'sparing the rod and spoiling the child'. I think she saw that, so far from the recipe working with this offspring of hers, it only made him unbearable. The 'rottennesses' from then on were accordingly mild by comparison. They included dismissal from meals, banishing to my room for longish periods, bible-searching impositions (how I loathed those abominable rummagings and scrabblings into the dust-heap of Holy Blasted Scripture!), and reiterated tight-lipped pronouncements that I lacked natural affection. Like hell, I did! Always it was the affront to love, the insult, the indignity, the humiliation which got to me, rather than the penalty itself. No doubt I asked, in disobedience and rudeness, for nearly all I got. But not quite. Here's an instance. My sister Freda has a scarlet birthmark on her forehead, which she manages to hide by arranging her hair to cover most of it. Well, Mother made out that I was responsible for this blemish on an otherwise handsome face. It seems that, in a fit of temper, I hit her on the belly while she was pregnant with Freda. Now Freda happens to be only just over a year younger than I am: which means that here was I, at six or seven, being charged with a violent crime committed when I was all of one year old! Which, I considered, was going too far, and certainly wasn't conducive to warmth between my sister and me. I leave aside that fact that — as I now know but my mother didn't know — these so-called birthmarks and nevi aren't got that way.

The last MRR episode I remember distinctly was less clear-cut but all the more significant and subtle than the others. I had been staying for a fortnight with my worthy and well-liked Aunt Mabel and family, in the neighbouring town of Stowmarket (PBs all, but of the better — i.e.,

Douglas approving — kind), and enjoying there an unfamiliar expansion and ease.

Here were new joys and a new dignity — I was asked and not ordered to do things, I was actually listened to, I was allowed to soak for ages in a proper H. and C. bathtub. The freedom from that unremitting surveillance and criticism, imposed by word and look and gesture, left me lightsome and open and six inches taller — and, I hoped, from now on a force to be reckoned with. But alas, the fortress fell at the first assault. I was no match for Her. With unerring instinct, Mother identified this mood as what it was — my unilateral declaration of independence — and started sanctions at once. I was in a trance, she said, as if it were a wickedness; and she was right, if to be more self-aware and self-sufficient, and not less so, can be read as a trance state. In any case, she knew exactly how to make me snap out of it. Snap into a smallness and a meanness. In all sorts of ways, big and petty, blatant and concealed, she resumed her domination and I resumed my resentment — recording, a Junior but industrious Arch-angel, her sins, in my MRR Domesday Book. As if, at the conclusion of the age, secula seculorum, she would be made to answer for every one of them. And, if not punished for it, at least made to blush scarlet, and tremble, tremble...

Yet no doubt she loved her firstborn, after her own fashion. Conceivably, in some senses and at some times, just as much as my father did. And no doubt, at some level, I loved her. But the mutually inflicted pain stood always in the way of love's conscious emergence and expression. At nineteen, I left home, and in the years that followed — up to her death when I was forty-two, and beyond that — I spared her little thought, and (as I now realise at long last) mistook our physical and mental distancing for reconciliation and healing. In fact, the wound has stayed wide open all these years. Only now, as I write this autobiography, do I clearly recognise and feel the hurt, the mortification, the debilitating effect of that long-drawn-out mother-son trauma. Only now do I clearly perceive how at last it comes to be healed. Altogether healed, healed *mystically*. As I shall explain presently, showing precisely how it's never too late to have a wonderful mum.

5. Experiences of the Fourth Kind

Increasingly I'm having a difficulty here, an *embarras de richesses*.

Now that I come to relive — as never before, oh never! — those early years, all manner of long-buried memories keep springing up, some joyful, some tearful, some grotesque, some disgraceful, some hilarious. And all of them, no doubt, in some more or less roundabout way, connected with the specifically mystical experiences of my childhood and later years. However, my concern isn't to draw on that memory-bank exhaustively and for its own sake, but just sufficiently to provide a background against which those mystical experiences can be made sense of and, at least in some degree, understood.

For the moment, then, that background has been sufficiently sketched in. It remains for me to conclude this part of the chapter (which, you'll recollect, is telling Complexiton's story) by painting in the foreground what I'm going to call *experiences of the fourth kind*.

Let me explain:

Philosophers talk of three values — truth, beauty, and goodness. I say there's a fourth — the mystical — which can neither be dispensed with nor assimilated to the others. On the one hand, some things are true and beautiful and good without being mystical: they come with a wind that's warm and health-giving, but it blows from the hills we know, not from the Unknown Country beyond them. For example, it is wonderfully good that Mr. Jones, who can ill afford it, gave £100 for famine relief in Somalia: also it was a beautiful deed in an often ugly world, and truly it happened; but I can find nothing mystical about it. On the other hand, some things are mystical without being true, or conspicuously beautiful, or conspicuously good: rather they are neutral in these respects. For example, it may well not be true that Robert Frost, on a particular snowy evening, stopped his little horse by the woods; and I'm pretty sure that the little horse didn't wonder what was going on. Nor, even if everything did happen exactly as Frost said it did, was it a good and beautiful happening. What event could be less remarkable? Yet, quite unaccountably, Frost's poem is a mystical stunner. It leaves one weak-kneed and tottering with admiration, gives one the shivers. Full-throat, it sings of that Other Country, in a language that is untranslatable. Of course, the mystical may also be true and beautiful (like the sight and the smell of mimosa in the shop at 107 High Street), or true and beautiful and good (like some of my father's many little kindnesses to me), but that's no reason for confusing the fourth value with the others. There is a line, a watershed, a Great Divide, on one side of which the rainfall of experience flows into an unmystical Atlantic, and on the other into a mystical Pacific; and it may be a breath of a breath of wind that settles which ocean a particular raindrop ends up in. For me as a child, as now, it's touch and go whether an autumn leaf on the pavement, or the inside of a tulip, or a gas flame, or the apple-green streak in a sunset, or a snatch of distant music, or a line of Shakespeare, or an unexpected gesture of game-free genuineness and love, or what-have-you, happens to shine with that fourth light. And clearly that what-have-you doesn't *need* any story — false or true — to tell, or any good cause to further, or any beauty to elaborate, in order to conduct you to the highest peaks of mystical experience. It's self-sufficient. In fact, some experiences of the fourth kind aren't nice at all. A few could fairly be described as horrifying — as we're about to see. So it is for me now, and so it was for me as a child.

Those peaks belong to a mountain range of indefinite extent. Nevertheless I see six or seven of them standing out from the rest.

Here they are, more or less in ascending order. No: that won't quite do. They make up a single pattern against the sky, a grand design to which each makes its unique contribution.

6. A Survey of Mystical Peaks

(i) The body

The idea has got around that the mystical and the physical are poles apart. If that's so, they are polar extremes which meet and unite. For me, at least, they are inseparable. One of the surest marks of the truly mystical is that it's felt all over one's body — a subtle but pervasive tingle or through-and-through liveliness, a frisson or shudder of delight, and specially an uplifting and exaltation, as if one were an outsize iron filing or an even-more-elongated iron figure by Giacometti, being pulled heavenwards by God's almighty magnet. I don't care if my spirituality is as holy as an Exclusive PB prayer meeting, if it lacks this body-tone, this coiled-spring feeling (and, by God, how those meetings did lack just that!) it's de-spirited and unholy-some stuff, and light-years distant from what I'm on about here. How well I remember, by contrast, racing home from school in the unreligious snow, the wind smacking my face, feeling as tall as the sky and as swift as a sea gull soaring there! Every nerve dissolved into pure joy.

It's true, I grant you, that the varieties of mystical experience that follow are less overtly physical than this, nevertheless all participate in the same singular ecstasy, which is not the same as a feeling of radiant health. Obviously it can't be: ill people are at least as open to experiences of the fourth kind as fit people are. No: it's more a sense of well-being than of being well. More like being hi-fi, finely tuned and on the qui vive and ready for anything, delicately yet firmly poised. Paradoxically, it's at once a feeling of concentration, of being unusually *recollected* and together, and one of unlimited expansion outwards and upwards: of combined implosion and explosion. As they say, it holds your shit together: as I say, your shit, held together in this mystical fashion, is instantly transmogrified — along with its delighted proprietor — into a pure and worldwide brightness. I'm not imagining this: it's a fact! Now there's sewage disposal for you! But these and any other descriptions, though they hint at it, are really beside the point. Here is a wind from an Unknown Country, a tangible and scented and cloud-chasing gale which nevertheless blows from a territory that can be found on no map; but yet is the realest of the real, one's very own dear and native land. The land whose natives aren't cowed and got down by life, who don't find themselves under the weather, but *walk tall* — truly a race of giants.

Flabby mysticism (of which there are huge quantities around) is mystical only in the popular sense of that which mystifies and obscures with roseate clouds, and relaxes one's attention and dissipates one's energy and blunts one's intelligence. It's scatter-brained, if not plain scatty. The real article is as taut and firm, as keenly discriminating as a Samurai's sword. I have long recognised as truly mystical the experience that is also bodily in this strictly indefinable sense, and come to value its physicalness or incarnation very highly. And the foundations of that recognition and that valuation were laid down years before that so-memorable racing through the snow, getting on for three-quarters of a century ago.

(ii) Colour

Experiences of the fourth kind are unpredictable, never within your control, never certain but always liable to happen. They take you by the shoulder when you least expect them, and shake you and shake you. They surprise. Just about anything is capable of bringing you stop-press news of Home. The merest whiff of violets; even — on some rare occasion — the word *violet*, perhaps. But I have to say that it is their *colour* which is most apt to pull off the magic trick for me. Brilliant colours have a way of trumpeting the presence of their Royal Source, of manifestly taking fire at its Fire, of bawling out a wordless secret that I need to know about the Nature of Things, about the Cosmic Paint Box itself. Not for me those powdery pastel shades beloved of some interior decorators, not for me just any old patch of strong and pure colour, either; but that colour backed with the right deep texture, as in the wing of the Small Copper and the Peacock butterflies, and the flags of the nations ablaze in a stiff breeze outside the U.N. on a brilliant morning, and the stunning sight of lobelia when the sunshine strikes at a certain angle. A blue flame that scorches the patient air.

But this isn't all. As if generous areas of such powerful and richly textured colour weren't quite marvellous enough, something more marvellous still may be added when these colours shade by imperceptible degrees into one another — as in Japanese goldfish, dewdrops on grass in the low sun, the petals of zinnias and some mesembryanthemums, and the wing-cases of the beetle that's well-named *Chrysis Ignita*... I've just been to the next room to admire once more Marc Chagall's 'Violinist' — the player's pink-merging-into-white trilby, his yellow-merging-into-orange-into-grey-green fiddle, his shades-of-myrtle-green face gashed with one twisted red lip. For no reason I can figure out, this gradual changing over or vignetting of colours is more than magical, more than mystical in any ordinary sense of the word. From my earliest childhood it has told me something about the Godhead and myself and the world which could be told in no other way. How curious, how beautiful, that His Majesty should condescend to a dewdrop and stuff it full of a glory that Heaven is too small and low-key to hold. I like him for that!

Down by the beach, by the wreck of the Spider — the fishing vessel I'd watched being driven ashore in a gale — I discovered a mine of jewels. Red and blue and green and amber they were; and with them I worked a powerful magic, creating red and blue and green and amber worlds, just as I pleased. Naturally those jewels were for me much more precious than all the toys I owned — or rather (as a fairly toy-less PB child) didn't own, and didn't much want, seeing that none had a hint of this world-transforming power. But alas an ogress called Miss Chipperfield, my teacher at dame school, detected and confiscated them, with some drivel about how naughty and dangerous it was to go round with jagged bits of glass from a filthy rubbish dump in my pocket — to say nothing of the damage to my nice knickers. Tears of bereavement and fury followed, as my jewels were dropped, with gestures of disgust, in the dustbin.

I must have been about five or six then. When I had reached twice that age, a sympathetic Brother from Norwich presented me with a collection of real, though tiny, emeralds and rubies. They were a joy, though far too small, of course, to open up emerald and ruby worlds.

My standby was the port and starboard lights of the harbour and the ships at night, and in winter the stained-glass window of the church seen from the street when an evening service was going on inside. Nobody could steal those jewels from me. What's more, they had the lovely advantage of being self-luminous, brilliantly lit from within. They began my lifelong love affair with coloured lights of all kinds. I'm thinking specially of the New Jerusalem seen from Heaven, the mystical vision which they pooh poohed and wrote off as New York seen from a plane flying at 5,000 feet at night, and not worth a second glance. And of what, down on earth, they said were perfectly ordinary traffic lights and neon signs reflected in perfectly ordinary wet asphalt streets at night, and what's all the fuss about? — but I saw as a city running with fiery green and blue and red and orange and amber blood. And of those purple lights they line runways with, fitting preview of the heavenly scenes air travellers are about to visit — if they choose to do so.

(iii) Music

Musically speaking, I was a wretchedly disadvantaged child.

Yet there was enough music around to hint at the revelation that was to come when, having reached twenty-one and escaped from the Brethren, I heard a competent singer and a competent choir and a competent orchestra for the first time. There were, as I said, a little way back, those bouncing, thumping, naughty sounds issuing from the Cosy Corner and the Spreadeagle; there were the occasional drum-and-fife band marching down the High Street at the head of yet another contingent of troops destined for the trenches, and in the summer, before and after the War, a brass band tooting away distantly on the pier. Sometimes angel voices could be heard as one walked by the church on the way to and from Meeting. And once, just once, I managed to attend a school concert without being found out. My ecstasy, my empathy with those divinely inspired young bassoonists and trombonists and frenetic bangers of drums was immeasurable. Every particle of me took off. Afterwards — all sense of sin forgotten — I wanted to clap forever.

My first lengthy exposure to non-PB music — and indeed non-PB life — was the time I spent in hospital recovering from an operation for appendicitis. (It left a huge and hard-to-heal wound, apparently inflicted with a table knife — I'm still proud of it.) In all sorts of ways it was the best fortnight of my young life, partly because it was the revelation of an unexpected world, and partly because even Mother — bearing daily gifts of calves'-foot jelly — melted and relaxed her pressure. Though scarcely eight, I was put in a ward with wounded soldiers who — besides being awe inspiring characters with gripping and shocking tales to tell — played a gramophone incessantly. A tinny and scratchy old thing it was, and unaccountably there emerged from its huge throat only one tune. I could hum it to you still. Here are the lovely words, just as I heard them:

> If by you and you, hou,
> If by you and you hou, you hou, hou,
> And this I want to hou...

Not one of the higher peaks of mystical experience, I hear you comment. I tell you that for me it was what Mahayana Buddhists call a *dharani*, a piece of sacred gobbledegook well able to carry me, however briefly, to the Other Shore.

It was the first of my still-growing collection of pieces — a witches' brew of musical experiences that, independent of all rationale and merit and good taste, are potentially of the fourth kind. Included in the mix are the traditional theme in Berlioz' *Les Francs Juges*, where the accused gives up struggling and accepts his fate; Herb Alpert's Tijuana Brass rendering of *Mexican Shuffle* and *Up Cherry Street*; Peter, Paul, and Mary's *Where have all the Flowers Gone?*; Harry Belafonte's *Island in the Sun*; Blondie's *Heart of Glass*, with its excellent words; and Boney M's wonderful *Rivers of Babylon*. I put it to myself: are these last, after all, so very different in substance from a number of Mozart arias, from Stravinsky's *Pulcinella* and much of *Petrushka*, and all manner of classical pieces which have this same precious capability of making this world all right by uniting it to that world, of bringing out in a sudden blaze that fourth value? Who cares about aesthetic proprieties when such an issue is at stake? A mere sniff of that country — whether in cathedral or concert hall or disco is of no consequence — can suddenly suffuse and transfigure this one.

Not that playing any of these pieces on my record player

can be counted on to work this transfiguration. Of course not, any more than listening to Gregorian plainchant is always a confirmed economy-class ticket to Heaven. But it's a standby, and one may well be lucky.

(iv) Words

In the beginning was the Word. And the Word spoke of the fourth value.

How astonishing it is that a noise and sequence of noises, a string of sounds which developed out of hisses and howls and grunts and gurgles, should be able to say infinitely more than they purport to say: that they should sing! What a matter for thankfulness it is that human speech should be so infected with a value that lies beyond all humanness and all speaking!

I was brought up on the Bible, and still am apt to recite large chunks of it, given the slightest excuse. Its hold on my thinking and feeling will be relaxed only when I die. What a model for speech and writing is here, with its directness and economy, its ear for the right sound sequence, its command — when occasion and topic demand it — of phrases and sentences and verse on verse which (like that racing through the snow) take over one's whole body.

In fact, there were for me, and still are, not one but two kinds of mystical thrill which the Bible invokes. I'll call them the general kind, and the particular kind. One example of the former will be enough:

> Remember now thy Creator in the days of thy youth, while the evil days come not, nor the years draw nigh, when thou shalt say, I have no pleasure in them.

While the sun, or the light, or the moon, or the
stars, be not darkened, nor the clouds return after
the rain:

In the day when the keepers of the house
shall tremble, and the strong men shall bow
themselves, and the grinders cease because they
are few, and those that look out of the windows
be darkened,

And the doors shall be shut in the streets, when
the sound of the grinding is low, and he shall rise
up at the voice of the bird, and all the daughters
of musick shall be brought low;

And when they shall be afraid of that which
is high, and fears shall be in the way, and the
almond tree shall flourish, and the grasshopper
shall be a burden, and desire shall fail:

because man goeth to his long home, and the
mourners go about the streets:

Or ever the silver cord be loosed, or the golden
bowl be broken, or the pitcher be broken at the
fountain, or the wheel broken at the cistern.

Then shall the dust return to the earth as it was:
and the spirit shall return to God who gave it.

I don't pretend to understand the imagery of this superb
passage. Nor, in order to find it deeply mystical, do I need to
do so, any more than I need to understand the physics of light
in order to find the combination of black and yellow and red

— as in the Belgian flag — to be more mystical than, say the French tricolour. As for its overall message, why it's the same as this book's overall message, which is that we grown-ups are in all manner of trouble so long as we bury our childhood alive. To be innocent of this horrible crime, and to rediscover the life of our present life, we must go back to its beginnings... Yes: I know: what this passage from *Ecclesiastes* means *to me* is what I *make* it mean. The Devil (as my mother often had occasion to point out) quotes scripture to justify anything. In fact, one of the minor arts I learned from the Brethren is the judicious selection and editing of scripture — in my case, eventually, the scriptures of all the principal religions — to fit what, in my guts, I know to be true. I am unrepentant. Appreciating the mystical content of any text is quite unlike appreciating its theological or moral content. It's more like training a dog. From the start you have firmly to establish who is master and who is pet. Zen masters tell the same story. You just have to manipulate the sutras: because, if you don't, the darn things will manipulate you. Or words to that effect. The mark of true mystics is that they don't speak in their human capacity: it's the indwelling Spirit, or Christ, or Atman-Brahman, or Buddha Nature, which speaks through them. No wonder, then, that they come out with this little respect for sacred texts. In short, God's even cleverer than the Devil at monkeying with his own Holy Word.

My second or particular example of the mysticism of the Bible provides the most striking example of this mastery.

From as early as I can remember, I was unaccountably excited by such first-person-singular texts as:

> I am the resurrection and the life, and he who
> believeth in me shall never die

I am the alpha and the omega, the first and the
last, the bright and morning star

I will overturn, overturn, overturn, until he come
whose right it is, and I will give it to him.

Behold, I come quickly

At the time I had no idea why the silent recitation of these
statements should be as thrilling as that race through the
snow, and the bang, thump, clang of that Cosy Corner music:
with even more, perhaps, of the accompanying *exaltation*. For
exaltation it was and is, just as if I were the subject of those
grand assertions! As if I were the august Speaker, Himself!
As if I were the resurrection and the life!

Terrible thought! Consciously to entertain such a notion as
a child — a PB child, at that — would, of course, have been
an unthinkable blasphemy. All the same, the identification
of that I AM with this I am was as covertly certain then as
it is overtly certain now. The uplift, the happiness, the rock-
like finality don't change with the years. Whether explicit or
implicit, it's the steady and lifelong conviction of one's true
Identity. A conviction I won't defend here at length, except
to say this: Why of course I AM is one and indivisible, and
for me to imagine otherwise — to go about setting up shop
independently to pretend I have a private little *I am* of my
own here, aside from that grand *I AM* — now *that's* the
wicked blasphemy! In the words of St Catherine of Genoa,
'my Me is God, and I recognize no other'. This is the quintes-
sential combination of the utmost exaltation with the utmost
humility. How thankful I am that my upbringing lent itself
so well to both! The way I put it to myself much later was: *To*

be saved is to be Him. If I were to cover this house I'm living in with graffiti, its sole message and signature would be the very first of my names: not *I am Douglas Edison Harding*, or *I am Douglas*, but plain *I am.* The rest are nicknames. And deciduous.

(v) Self-giving Love

I AM doesn't come cheap. Its very nature is to give itself, which is expensive. It is what it is and complete, not by dominating and gobbling up other *I ams*, but by making way for them, by disappearing in their favour. In the eyes of the Brethren, of course, like all other evangelicals, the sacrifice of their Lord on the cross was the unique expression and paradigm of this self-giving love, and the centre-point of history. Yet it left me lukewarm. The divine self-sacrifice didn't move me as it should have done — maybe because I tried so hard (specially at the Breaking-of-Bread Meeting) to return the Lord's love, maybe because I was too divine and insufficiently human, and maybe also because it all happened so long ago. No: it was more ordinary and comprehensible gestures — often the most commonplace and trivial acts of kindness — that evoked the fourth value and moved me to tears. A child helping an old woman across the street, my father comforting me after a tumble; and later — and not at all trivial — the story of the first Christmas at the Front, when German and British soldiers sang carols for one another and exchanged gifts.

I suspect that I owe to the Brethren, and specially to my father, one of the most precious of all gifts: namely, the ineradicable conviction that, back of all things, and despite every grim indication to the contrary, shines the noonday sun of Love Absolute; and that is why, when here and there a pinpoint of its light briefly shines through all obscuring clouds, the effect can be so out-of-proportion to its immediate and seeming cause. Why, some would say, a cup of cold water given in the name of that Love can so gratify both the giver and the taker.

I've already mentioned that I managed to smuggle Dickens into the house under the guise of homework, and exercising due care not to be seen reading him with any avidity. Serious Dickensian studies were for the privacy of my bedroom; or, more safely, the W.C. Well, the first of his novels that I read was *The Tale of Two Cities*, a story of surrender and self-sacrifice at many levels, culminating in Sidney Carton's giving his life for his 'enemy', his rival in love. Victorian melodrama at its most sentimental, no doubt, but it devastated me for days after the reading of it. You may remember how the scene is set in Paris at the height of the Revolution; and how Sidney, the dissipated and rejected suitor of Lucie, takes the place of her husband Charles, who lies in prison awaiting execution by guillotine. And how he was sustained in this heroic act by repeating to himself the text:

> I am the resurrection and life, saith the Lord:
> he that believeth in me, though he were dead,
> yet shall he live:
> and whoever liveth and believeth in me
> shall never die.

Curiously enough, it took Dickens in the W.C., hidden from PB eyes, to bring this biblical passage to life — and more than life — for me. Directly after finishing his novel, I had to meet a cousin at the railway station. If there ever was a heaven on earth, it was there. It was that station, on that summer day seventy years ago. The shabby grey-brick premises of the Great Eastern Railway were Paradise, and the smell of fairly fresh fish, and the sound of steam engines in the height of their furore, were the smell and the sound of the Love that has all because it gives all, and invades all because it underlies all.

(vi) From what it is to that it is

This, the sixth and last peak of the range of mystical experiences recollected from my childhood, sports a very different shape and colour from the others. It stands out prominently against the sky, well apart from them. In fact, it's a question whether it belongs to the same mountain range, at all. As you will presently see for yourself.

You'll already have gathered that I was a cocksure lad, as well as a complicated one. I was so intimidated by Holy Scripture that it structured my young life, yet so unintimidated that I coolly revised the first chapter of Genesis. Convinced that it didn't go back far enough, I ended by rewriting it altogether. Somewhat along the following lines:

In the beginning was nothing whatever. And no-one to note the fact.

In the beginning was no God to create the heavens and the earth. He came later. They came later still.

First things first.

In the beginning all was silent and still, without form and void.

No-one at home — and no home. No status quo, let alone anything or anyone to upset it. This was natural, exactly as it should be...

And then, for no reason, the Irregularity happened, the

Absurdity, the Impossibility. God, who didn't yet exist, said 'Let there be God!' And there was God! *Whoopee!*

And he saw that he was very good. And *very* unnatural. Not just an ordinary Fluke, but one so freakish that it freaked itself into existence. Hugely he enjoyed the fact that, in creating himself before he was there to do so, he had indeed pulled a fast one. So fast that it preceded itself. After which feat the creation of billions of inhabited universes was a piece of cake, no trouble at all.

God is still in a state of shock, delighted shock at his own continuous self-invention, against impossible odds. He will never have any idea how he pulls off the trick. Unlike him, people — including countless millions of his so-called worshippers — aren't at all puzzled. They have him taped, crediting him with a virtue that's really a dreadful defect, they imagine that Being *has* to be, that God is necessary, and therefore as un-mysterious as up and down and left and right. The back-handed compliment of all time! What can he say to these people who take him for granted as the supreme *fait accompli*, as the one who, because he's *obliged* to exist, is entitled to no admiration for doing so, let alone adoration? Only this: 'You, you who profess to honour me, strip me of my brightest robe and richest crown. That hymn you sing, "My God, how wonderful thou art!" is irony and mockery. You have made me so comprehensible, so commonplace. Poor silly dears — what you are missing! Your worship is so shallow, so beside the point, so unrewarding. Besides, you are cheating yourselves of the keenest joy of your life, which is the realisation that your wonder at my self-invention is no human wonder, but my very own. Here, you are God bowing to God, God overwhelmed by God's impossibility, and our joy is one and the same joy. Given this divine joy, which is upstream of all worlds, what is the sorrow those worlds are full of?'

Yes of course: this is mighty subtle stuff for a teenager, let alone a young child! Naturally I grant that the way I have just put the matter is anything but childlike: it has the benefit of a lifetime's brooding upon it. But the substance itself, the wonder and the delicious bafflement, not only stem from my childhood but are forever rooted in it. How many children, when informed that God made the world, ask (or would ask if they dared) who made God; and how few of them, growing up, go on asking that question? The rules of the human club forbid it. As for myself, I can put no date on the beginning of this metaphysical wonder (leaden phrase for a mood so soaring!), or on the stages of its development from a plain 'Why is there anything at all?' to this irreverent shot at re-writing *Genesis* 1. Ultimately, I suspect, this variety of mystical experience is not in time at all. In any case I can think back to no moment when it was altogether absent from my life. And now — if I pray at all — it is that I shall never get over it. Why so? Because God and his chief glory are in it, the God who is so astonished that I'll wager his eyebrows have taken off altogether.

(vii) Faces

I am choosing these peaks — these representative experiences of the fourth or mystical kind — from a range which includes many others that aren't necessarily less prominent, a range that actually is limitless. In fact, there exists no feature of the landscape which cannot, when viewed in a new light or from a new angle, reveal itself as yet another peak — in shape and colouring unique and maybe grotesque, but lit with the same Light as all are. Additionally, there's an indefinite number of prominences which — because they happen to loom up less frequently in one's life rather than because they are less awesome — I've omitted from my list. By way of illustration, here is one I had thought of leaving out but now include: an oddly disturbing experience whose mystical content, again, is out of all proportion to its non-mystical container, to the occasion itself. Though this particular instance belongs to my adulthood, it arises out of similar experiences in my childhood. So much so that it feels like a reversion to it:

The scene is the courtyard of the Palazzo Pitti in Florence one summer night. A knock-about show is afoot. It's in Italian, my seat's not a good one and I have only the vaguest notion of what's going on. People next to me chatter, and make disparaging remarks about the show. But what do I care? The performers — Scaramouche and so on, traditional characters from the Comedia del Arte, have a certain fascination. But it's their *masks* — those bulging and twisted and squashed and elongated faces, painted in strong luminous colours, which hit me like shrapnel. Specially those long drawn-out chinless noses. Or are they chinless beaks? Chinless, anyway. And shrapnel? Oh hell, here I am remembering what I am unable to forget: that at the Front it occasionally happened that a soldier's lower jaw was blown off; and he survived fully conscious, while strong men around him fainted with the shock of what they saw. I'm thinking of some pictures I have seen, and can't un-see. I'm thinking of how, at twenty-five, I somehow contrived to fall smack on my face while skating. There was I, just feeling numb up there, it was the others that got the jar. That melange of broken teeth and bits of lip and bloody moustache was the other skaters' problem, not mine at all. There they were, gazing spellbound and frozen and on the point of passing out, into another world... Also I'm thinking that, whether the face I see in my mirror is finally disposed of by burial or by burning, it's due briefly to revert to the way it was on that day on the ice at Constable's Flatford Mill. To be reduced again to something like that — or worse.

All of which goes to show, again, how very far from good and beautiful these experiences of the fourth kind may be.

Having broached the subject of faces, I can hardly let it go at that. So much of this book is going to be about these, the most haunted and fraught of all the mystical objects the world is packed with. And of course I've no intention of ignoring the other side of the physiognomic medal — their mystical awesomeness, which is the obverse and complement of the mystical awe-fulness we've just been looking at. Let me illustrate, or at least hint at that awesomeness and glory, if I can.

The scene is a special PB gathering for the reading and discussion of Scripture, being held in Cambridge. Around a couple of hundred Brothers and Sisters have turned up, of whom I recognise perhaps a quarter. There are two or three big-wigs, who dominate the discussion: bishops and archbishops are less revered in their congregations than are these Top Brethren, in and out of Meeting. There's a sprinkling of children salivating in anticipation of the cherry-rich Dundee cake which is for us much of the attraction of these district get-togethers. Meantime it's those faces which grip me. Most of them are rather pursy and prim and dour, some are downright forbidding and a few are lovely. How all-revealing they

are, how transparent, how unsuccessful at hiding the quality
— the misery, the madness, the meanness, the complacency,
the tenderness, the ecstasy — the peculiar quality of the PB
life going on there! In varying degrees hypnotic in their fascination these faces keep their hold on my rapt attention, so
that I don't hear (and don't want to hear) what they are saying.
Nothing mystical about them, however. (Not, of course, that
I have this word, or any word, for it.) Except for one face,
belonging to Mr Wilson. I remember that my mother disap-
proves of Mr. Wilson: he used to be a well-off factory manager
(she says), but threw up his job in order to wander around
the Highlands and Islands telling people how much Jesus
loves them, and leaving his wife and two daughters to live
unprovided for in some wretched cottage. Mother's censure
only fuels my admiration. Looking at him, I know what the
Transfiguration on the Mount must have been like for those
amazed disciples. Here's a face that shines like the tremendous
sun of a brighter and kinder world. A luminary that can't
help but light up my own face with its seraphic fire, so that
in some inexplicable way, a black-haired and red-cheeked and
very un-saintly kid of ten *became* that snow-white haired and
pink-cheeked saint of sixty. I'm irradiated! I'm *wilsoned!* His
contribution to the holy talk is nothing special, his features
are not handsome, his voice is somewhat high pitched, and
it's accompanied by peculiar breathings in and out as if he
were sustained by another, a more rarified air. And there's
something about that face that says it all.

Recording here, after all those years, my recollection of it
I'm reminded of perhaps half a dozen other faces with that
same *je-ne-sais quoi* — that glow, radiance, serenity — perhaps shining is the least misleading word for it. The first face

is my father's, on occasions in and out of Meeting. Another is the face of a girl of six called Gretchen: I saw her twice in Denver, Colorado, six years ago. Another is the face of a by-no-means beautiful or scintillating woman of (I guess) around forty, whom I'm due to meet again in a few days time. There's a point in the *Paradiso* of Dante's *Divine Comedy* when he realises that he has ascended to a higher celestial sphere. How does he know that? Not by some interior effulgence, not by astronomical observation and reckoning. His clue is the new light that shines in the face of his lady: of Beatrice, his guide. The same Beatrice whose loveliness, when he first saw her on the bridge over the Arno, caused him almost to faint.

(viii) The face

Brief excursion into adulthood here, while I'm still on the subject of faces.

I picture to myself now my own Beatrice, my guide to Earth and the Heavens, and the many faces she has worn over the years — faces plain as well as beautiful, serious as well as smiling, of various ages and both sexes, but all of them aglow with the same serene light. And now they come together and merge in just one face, in what would be an identikit portrait except that it is incarnate, emerging as just one special face. Or, in a sense, two faces, a pair.

The first is lighting up every day and every hour of my life, and every fragment of my world. Just one particular woman's face, not youthful or beautiful by glossy magazine standards, by no means uniformly cheerful, at times tired-looking and even sombre — yet bringing to a head all the loveliness in the world. Such is its mysterious brilliance and penetrating power that it irradiates me through and through, dissipating all the darkness and heaviness here. And such is its gentleness that it does so quietly without the slightest dazzle or obtrusiveness. Her face is my stillness and my peace. The merest thought of her — let alone a sharp visualising — is enough to work this miracle of silent illumination. Unlit by that light, my life is a dimness, ungenerous and chill, a shivering life half felt and half lived, a life in part missed out on.

Need I add that it is a light that shines *for me*? With mild astonishment I note that it doesn't do so for others — at least not in anything like the same degree. For most of her friends as well as acquaintances she has, I gather by small signs, why yes a nice face, with a certain kindliness and charm for sure, but nothing to write home about. A blind world it is! But what do I care, who see?

Whose face it is I shall not say, for a bunch of good reasons. Anyway the official name it bears is quite irrelevant to the story I'm telling here. So I'm christening this lady — this mystical guiding star and spiritual love of mine (how thin and bloodless and shop-soiled this talk is, compared with the reality!) — rechristening her Eyebright, a name lifted from my *Head Off Stress*, where she figures as the one who, among all her companions, sees most steadily into her interior transparency and no thingness. Accordingly this name could not be more fitting. For Eyebright — whether that fictional personage or this real-life one — is pre-eminently a seer, a push-over for the mystical vision, a natural, to the manner born, by temperament and inclination one of the world's illuminati, if ever there were such. It is this grace, this best of gifts, which is the secret at the heart of her loveliness.

Eyebright, to envisage you now is pure joy, undiminished by all those miles and days that part us! Joy that wants nothing that you don't give, in full flood, at this very moment. In it that double-distancing telescopes and collapses.

And, as I say, your face has another aspect and another name. It merges into a remoter face, the face of my mother. Her face as she first gave it to me. The face that was my first love. The face which was — no matter how unfocused — all the world to me, my original *other*, my earth and my heaven.

And now, suddenly, thanks to Eyebright, my mother and I are at last reconciled. This is more than mutual forgiveness and the rediscovery of love. It's as if my Domesday Book, that record of Mother's Rottenness, were instantly transformed into a record of Mother's Radiance, a holy mother-son icon. And a new ease and health and freedom, as well as joy, supervene, as the long handicap of mother-son alienation is finally overcome. The fact that my mother's face, initially angelic, too soon became for me witchlike and sometime demonic — this sad fact only serves to highlight its present transfiguration. Restored now to its original perfection (shall I call it tender, alight with all the beauty of the cosmos?) — I don't want to embellish it, or nail down and crucify the mystery with fine words. Enough to say that here for me isn't so much a peak mystical experience as a range of peaks, stretching into the blue distance. Thank God, I can no longer separate the light and the face of my Beatrice, alias Eyebright, from that on the faces of so many down the years; and none of it from the radiance on the face of my mother, as she looked down at the puckered and rubicund features of her firstborn.

Such is the tale of our reconciliation. I repeat: it's never too late to have the best mum in the world. And, till I find this out, till I learn from Eyebright the present secret of it, I didn't know what a peak mystical experience could be, at its loftiest and grandest, in the warm glow of dawn and sunset no less than in its snow-white noonday purity.

3. THE CHILD THAT I AM

1. The Valley Experience

How odd that the Beauty which reduces all beauty to prettiness — that encapsulates the Poignancy and Mystery of the world — should be contained in this insignificant, curiously rubberised, fast-perishing, and potentially awful fragment of the world, called the human face! And that's just for starters! Helen's face launched a thousand ships.

There's a Face which launches a thousand universes, just like that! What's more, it's your True Face and it's my True Face. The Face we're now coming to. The Face of the Simpleton. The Face that is never there, always here. Never another's, always one's own.

In fact, we have come to a variety of mystical experience which isn't within a million miles of belonging to the mountain range we've just been exploring. Which isn't a *peak* experience at all, but — precisely the contrary — a *valley* experience. Or rather, *the* Valley Experience. It's unique. Not just very different from all other mystical experiences, but in all respects their opposite. Strictly speaking, therefore, *mystical* is the worst of misnomers here. As silly to class it with them as to call black a shade of white, or silence a note on the scale. Absurd, also, to award it any value of our fourth kind. Nor will it do to set up a fifth value-pedestal to display this experience on. A pit, or bottomless and dry well, would be more fitting. In a very precise sense, it is valueless.

Or, better, put it like this: its immense value is that, though perfectly real, it is clean of all values, adorned (and limited) by no qualities whatever. As we shall presently see.

So far however, you would be justified in dismissing this Valley Experience as a nonsense: as a non-experience which, if you could get it, wouldn't be worth having. Entirely justified and entirely wrong. In fact, it makes perfect sense , and is so ultra-valuable that it constitutes the indispensable Basis of all four of our values. If this book has a point and a raison d'être, if I have a song to sing here, it is the Valley Song, the song which strikes the deepest bass note. And that's not hard to strike. Nothing is so easy, so obvious , so accessible, as what's lowest — the lowest of the low, the bottom that is bottomless. So dead easy, so embarrassingly obvious, so instantly accessible at all times and so deep yet so natural in all places, that it gets less attention than the space we mill around in, or the white background of these black marks we're now pursuing from left to right across the page. What's most indispensable and most universal is most ignored.

A little way back, with the greatest of ease we shared it. We descended into that Valley together. We didn't make it to that place of truth: we didn't seek it or clamber down into it: we *tumbled* to it.

Following the direction of our pointing forefinger let's go back there. Let's have the enterprise and the simplicity to look again at what we're looking out of. Let's dare for a moment to cease overlooking the Looker — presence of or absence of...

Coming clean at last, submitting to and confessing to what does and what does not lie at the dead centre of our universe, at the place we're always at without noticing it, let's have — let's see, let's be — this unique and crucial Valley Experience. It's the one experience we can't get partially, or make a muck of. It's all-or-nothing. To have and to see and to be This is to do so to perfection. There are no degrees or aspects or stages of our Central Nature to be explored. Either we go down into this valley all the way, or else we stop altogether short at the brink. Or rather, we imagine we do. Just try avoiding this valley, if you can!

2. Re-infanting: The World Refurbished

The previous chapter told the story of the Complexiton whose adventures included the exploration of mystical peaks. This chapter looks at that story from the point of view of the valley-loving Simpleton, who doesn't so much explore the valley as make his home there and — in every sense of the word — is he homely!

My account, so far, of my childhood has been fairly honest, I'd say. As truthful, as free from deliberate distortion and suppression, as I can make it without trying desperately hard. All the same I have to admit that it's largely fictional, every bit as imaginary as it is actual-factual. Inevitably so. Out of a vast jumble of memories, I pick just a few because they interest me, and because they would interest you, and because of their mystical overtones — and not at all because they are representative of the rest. Moreover those select few I've totted up in clothes they certainly didn't sport at the time. Inevitably, again, all those so-called childhood experiences are adult experiences with a backward look, second-hand stuff, so much archeology. The exhibits are being viewed through the distorting lenses of a lifetime. As little hope of seeing those harbour lights I saw at four and of re-hearing that frenetic bang-bang school concert the way I heard it at eleven, as of seeing and hearing the Kalahari of the Bushmen or the Rome of Caesar.

All the same I stick to my self-appointed task in this book, as well as in the life I'm living, of *re-infanting*: of somehow and in some very real sense *being* the very same magician whose rubbish-dump jewelry turned the world red and blue and green in Lowestoft, way back in the second decade of this century. The very same one whose thaumaturgic powers have grown rather than petered out.

A tough assignment! How on earth is it possible to comply with it? Very, very easily! To tell the truth, there's no avoiding it, once I dare turn my attention round 180 degrees from the view to the Viewer.

The present Viewer is none other than that infant and that child, of three-quarters of a century ago.

Right here, closer to me than all else, is this ageless Peter Pan that I am. Here is the secret of eternal youth. Here is the perennial Viewer who never grows older by a split second, who is always the same and never shifts his viewpoint by an inch, or drops off to sleep for a second. Here is this Absolute Simplicity I've never ceased living from. The years have added nothing to what was here eighty years ago, and subtracted nothing. In this direction, being quite perfect from the start (what start?) I'm a case of totally arrested development. Thank the Lord.

In the opposite direction, of course, all is different as to detail. The coloured lights are no longer those of Lowestoft harbour, but of Los Angeles seen at night from the air, ten minutes before landing, briefly but gloriously living up to its name. The music I'm hearing isn't a pop number of 1916 hiccupping and spluttering from the horn of a wind-up gramophone with a worn-down needle, but Gustav Mahler smoothly flowing from beautiful boxes of tricks by Bang and Olufsen. The sunset I'm admiring now has a somewhat different scheme and cloud formation from any sunset I saw as a child, or — for that matter — from any sunset that ever was. Though the flowers are very similar to those early ones, they aren't the same flowers. In short and in general, what's *given* is always unrepeatable and fugitive, always changing always perishing and being renewed. Whereas what's *in receipt* of all that, what's taking it in here, never dies, never changes, never needs renewal. This alone is for ever the same, the same, the same. The same unstaling freshness.

Yes: but just a minute! What has been happening, throughout those years of unremitting change and sometimes spectacular development of the given, to the taker's sensitivity to it and enjoyment of it, to its overall quality *for me*? To my *feeling* for what's on show? Has what's taking in all this richness grown as it grew, or has it shrunk and withered? Hasn't the thrill died down? Hasn't the value leeched away somewhat? Haven't the impact, the charm, the sparkle, the novelty, the pungency — haven't these gone off a good deal? Hasn't the brooding light-over-all dimmed? I think that most people, and not just the poets who bemoan their lost childhood, would agree with Wordsworth that

> Not in entire forgetfulness,
> And not in utter nakedness,
> But trailing clouds of glory do we come
> From God, who is our home:
> Heaven lies about us in our infancy!
> Shades of the prison-house begin to close
> Upon the growing Boy,
> But he beholds the light, and whence it flows,
> He sees it in his joy;

The Youth, who daily farther from the east
Must travel, still is Nature's priest,
    And by the vision splendid
    Is on his way attended;
At length the Man perceives it die away,
And fade into the light of common day.

Many if not all of us have just enough recollection of the
clear air of the morning of our lives to convince us that our
afternoon and evening are — by contrast — obscured and
muffled by a shifting smog, of varying density and shades
of grey. Sadly, we have to admit that the shroud, ever more
stifling and restrictive, is settling upon us.

    Does it have to be like this? If so, why?

    That's life, they tell me. Such is the human condition, and
there's very little help for it. Not only does this person go off
and suffer the pains of slow psycho-physical deterioration,
but the scene follows suit. I'm born into a bright-shining and
magical world, and proceed to live and to die in a progressively
dull and boring commonplace one. There's no conditioner or
Buck-You-Up-O for my world, no universe tonic. No way to
clear, no way to thin, no way to prevent the descent of our
life's smog. They say...

    It's a lie! There is a remedy. There really is.

    Already we've been handed the prescription of that medi-
cine, have collected it from the pharmacist, have begun to take
it. Already we've learned — if not mastered — the science
and art of *re-infanting*, without sacrifice of any of the real
gains of our growing up: so that our adulting no longer has
to be our adulteration. All we have to do (said one who knew
what he was talking about) is to be converted, which means

turned round 180 degrees, and so become as little children.
Exactly as little children. It's simply a matter of attending
— in the right direction. With or without the help of this
in-pointing forefinger.

What does this mean precisely, at this moment precisely, for
me-as-I see-myself-to-be precisely? For me as bare accommodation for this scene.

It means that on the table over there are the carmine flowers of a polyanthus, lit up by the noonday winter sun and
glowing with a fire less dazzling but more fiery than the
sun itself. It means that the little plug at the non-business
end of the ball pen I'm writing this with, catching the sun,
is a blue flame of indescribable brilliance. It means that the
greeny-yellowy eye of the cat — of snow-white, pink-nosed,
loud-purring Mercedes stretched out at my side — is an
opening onto the extraordinariness of the world. It means
that the warm sun is fondling me with its old lovingkindness. It means that all this, and much more, is pervaded and
drenched with the exquisite smell — the natural perfume of
a *deodorizer*. The world cleansed of the acrid smell of smog.

All this for the simplest of simple reasons. *Because I let it in,
unhindered.* Because I've absolutely nothing here to keep this
glory out with, no screen to filter it through, no blind to pull
down on it, no smog to smudge and smear it with. Because
all that's needed, to be in receipt of this brightness and this
sweetness, is the absence here of any receiver, of anything
that's brightened and sweetened. The *conscious* absence. No:
I don't believe in this absence, this vacant accommodation
for all comers. I don't understand it. I don't feel it. I *see* it. I
see it here even more clearly (if that's possible) than I see
that flaming potted plant there. Therefore those flowers burn

and shine just as brightly as the flowers of my childhood. Therefore the world is as fresh and undimmed now as it was then. As it was when I was *for others* a two-year old, and *for myself* his absence. Call it alert capacity. *The pollution, the evil smelling smog that subsequently came between me and my bright world, was never THERE at all. It was right here, where it grew so thick that it condensed into a solid eight-inch ball of uncleanness.* Plumb in the centre of my world arrived *dirt* — the dirt that is matter in the wrong place. That head, which in its right place on the far side of the mirror, is pure treasure, trespassing on this side of it instantly becomes trash — trash which fouled and trashed my world. It was the bugbear and the misery of my adolescence and early manhood. And its seeing-off to where it belongs safely *behind* that protective glass, is my re-infanting, and at once my decontamination and my world's.

3. Re-infanting: The World Restructured

With that double brilliance, that double cleaning up, I'm off to a good start. A no-head start rather than a head start. But there's much more to re-infanting than that, much more to come, as we shall presently see.

   Whither is it fled, the visionary gleam?

   Where is it now, the glory and the dream?

asks Wordsworth. I answer: it is there where it always was. It has not fled, I blacked it out, I blocked it. But now dear God, in his lovingkindness, has knocked my block off. And I'm opened out onto a world that's not only gloriously refurbished but gloriously restructured from top to bottom. And a good thing, too!

   If it were just the brightness of my world as it is which

unites me, through the brightness of my world as it was, with my infancy, how could I be quite sure of my re-infanting? I need further evidence, preferably of a more measurable and objective kind. Well, I get it, abundantly. It crowds in upon me. Even more striking and convincing, far more precise and more readily verifiable than the renewed vividness of my world, is its restructuring, its remodelling in all respects. Repeat: in all respects. When the smog here clears, when the spherical mass of pollution, having come to a head here, is at last cleaned up by returning it to its proper place, why then I find myself back in the world I once lived in, the *given* world, the alive and true and *habitable* world, the *natural* world before it is denatured and torn apart and reduced to a charnel house of convenient fictions. The usefulness of which, though indubitable, is much exaggerated, and moreover is paid for very, very dearly. In fact, the price, which is set far too high, is negotiable — to say the least. Again, as we shall presently see.

I've been thinking about how best to introduce the main features of the world as thus demolished and rebuilt, and at the same time to give some idea of how they came about, and in what order. And I've decided that, since this is the story of one's re-infanting (more fully, of one's infanting, followed by de-infanting and re-infanting — a three-stage operation) it could fittingly take the form of a fairy tale. *Very* fittingly as it turns out, seeing that it takes us to the door of fairyland anyhow; and we might as well go right in as peek in. For the truth is that, ultimately, those three stages never happened. They were and are imaginary. In particular, as I've already said, our de-infanting is a make-believe, a dream developing into a nightmare, a species of monkey business. Yet, of course, it is a make-believe so well-made and so believable that the consequences could hardly be more disastrously realistic and far-reaching. And it's a monkey business so businesslike that it threatens to put straight dealing out of business altogether.

So fairytale let it be:

Monkey business

Once upon a time there lived a lad called Jack whose father was rich. Stinking rich, some said. Others, not exaggerating, all-the-perfumes-of-Arabia rich. In any case so wealthy and so open-handed, so much the loving father, that Jack's playroom was filled with every kind of toy imaginable and unimaginable. Spread out higgledy-piggledy on that vast and immaculate floor were playthings so ingeniously constructed and so exquisitely finished that they amounted to the genuine thing — in miniature. Repeat: the genuine thing. Double repeat: in miniature. Small here was beautifully normal, no less than normally beautiful. You could say, sacrificing grammar, real dinky. There were sparkling stars by the sprinkler full, a kind sun you could smother with a penny if ever you wanted to, frothy tumbling playful clouds, snow mountains, and aircraft of all sorts, none too large or hot or cold or speedy or pushy for comfort. There were neat little hills prinked out darkly with bonsai trees. There were dolls' houses perfect down to the last itsy-bitsy brick and tile and light-switch. Inside them lived dollies perfect down to the last teeny-weeny eyelash and wrinkle, coming and going, getting older all the while, laughing and crying real tears, and being nice and horribly nasty to one another. There were toy ships that sailed without any encouragement from Jack, all packed with little passengers carrying genuine luggage, and eating and drinking far more than was good for them. There were toy cars whose drivers' skill was incredible. And so on, and on. And all of these treasures spread out at random on the nursery floor, cheek-by-jowl, with a fine lack of order that wasn't in the least disorderly.

Naturally, perhaps, Jack found these wonderful treasures of his so absorbing that he quite lost himself in them, disappeared in their favour. I'm not saying that here was a small boy who for a time became the Moon or the tractor or the teddy he was busy with, and then briefly went back to being a small boy again before fastening onto some other treasure, but that he was never anything else than what happened to occupy him. That's the word I want — occupied him, to the exclusion of all the rest. And Jack was never unoccupied.

Now in the course of time one toy came to fascinate Jack more and more. It was a monkey. A pale-faced, grimacing specimen called Jacko. There were several reasons why Jacko got far more than his fair share of attention. In contrast to the other animals, he was devoted to his owner — so much so that he couldn't bear to take his eyes off him for a moment.

There Jacko was, always at hand and wide awake, never sleeping at his post, ever ready to have fun, playing the role of the perfect slave or tame genie. What's more, it wasn't all pretense. He was as able as he was eager to obey a good many of Jack's orders. Without knowing at all how he came by his skill as an animal trainer, Jack succeeded in getting Jacko to grin, pout, cry, stick his monkey tongue out, and do almost anything with his face except look away and close his eyes. So it's no surprise that Jack's pet monkey, trained to get up to so many tricks that his other pets couldn't or wouldn't even attempt, became his very, very special favourite.

As Jack grew older, his dad didn't exactly take away his toys. Nor did he exactly say: 'What a terrible mess!' No, he politely asked Jack to clear the nursery floor. 'The time has come,' he said, 'to put away childish things.' On the whole a dutiful and straightforward lad, Jack proceeded to do just that. Not any old how, not carelessly and at random, but systematically. Most of his bright-shining treasures he saw off skywards, dispatching galaxies and stars to the remotest heavens, planets and Sun and Moon to the nearer heavens. Clouds and aircraft also went some of the way up there. Mountains and hills and trees and houses and people and animals and plants and arms and legs were all duly sent off to their allotted regions — regions not so much up there as out there — till the nursery floor was wonderfully cleared, just as Father wanted.

And they didn't mind at all being sent away. Not one of them shrank with self-pity or swelled up with anger. They all stayed the same size as before — their very nice and proper size — and continued to behave themselves.

All the same, their departure meant that something very strange and important had happened. Jack's flat world had, almost overnight, becomes Jack's deep world. Oh so deep! Born into a two-dimensional universe, he had, with masterly magic — at Dad's request and as his accredited agent — created a three-dimensional one, and a fabulously populous one into the bargain. Before, as a young child, Jack had fingered the Moon, sifted stars through his hands like icing sugar, stroked those snowy peaks with never a suggestion of frost-bite, fondled rhinos and rubbed shoulders with tigers, and so forth. But now they had all left his nursery floor for depth upon depth of Space. How little damage they suffered on

the journey! How neatly they fitted into their places! What
a grand world they constituted! What a fine job young Jack
had done!

Nor was it that, in so cleverly and so unselfishly obeying
his father's request to put away childish things, he had lost
his treasures. Not at all. He kept up with them on their
outward journeys. Jack himself grew great depth, became
thoroughly two-dimensional. He didn't let one inch of space
or one second of time — or any distance at all that could
intervene between his nursery and his now far-flung treasures
— creep in to part himself from them. Without any difficulty at all he quietly exploded — whoosh! — to take in and
body forth the remotest and least populous of regions. Now
he was regal indeed, clothed with the heavens and crowned
with the stars. Less poetically, where there had been a lawn
there was a molehill, and the molehill became a mountain,
Mount Sumero, the World Mountain. Still less poetically,
from being a huge onion slice, Jack became a huge onion, the
World Onion. Talk about growing up and rising in the world,
talk about Jack and the Beanstalk: here's real exaltation! O
boy, O happy boy!

But, alas, very brief was Jack's glory. Something went
wrong, very wrong indeed. And it was all because of that
precious monkey of his.

What happened was this. Though obedient to Dad's orders
in general, Jack secretly ignored them in just one particular.
There was one treasure he couldn't bear to let go of at all.
Yes, it was his darling Jacko, the monkey whose devotion so
charmed and flattered him. He played a trick on Dad. Instead
of sending off Jacko with the rest, he held onto him more
tightly than ever: and released a mere picture of the monkey,

which he hung up there a yard or so away in place of the real thing, hoping against hope to deceive the Old Man. Ha, ha!

It was Jack's undoing. Not that Dad punished Jack for his disobedience, but that he punished himself — dreadfully. Just imagine — Jack *became* Jacko! World-maker and true son of his father, he made a monkey of himself. And stayed like that. And behaved like that, and much worse. And was very, very angry with himself. Or rather, with everyone but himself.

Though misplaced, his rage was certainly understandable. Before, he had been all his treasures and toys in turn, and there was safety in numbers. His good fortune and his freedom lay in the fact that they were so many, and so accessible, and so rich in their variety; and that, when he'd had enough of being just one member of that crowd, why he could instantly switch to being another and vastly different member. Bored with being animal, he could become, at the drop of the hat he never wore, vegetable or mineral. Sure enough, he had his favourites. He liked being the bulldozer more than the bulldozed, and the butterfly more than the caterpillar, and the caterpillar more than the leaf undergoing mastication. Nevertheless he could never endure to be anything — however splendid — for more than a few moments together.

But now all was changed. Daily he was stuck with Jacko, besotted with Jacko, for longer and longer periods, and in the end all the while. Not because Jacko wanted to stay, but because Jack — the victim of his addiction — wanted and needed to make sure he never got away. Jack had, you'll recollect, ceased for nearly all practical purposes to be Jack at all, and had become that monkey. So now it was that creature or nothing, and therefore a matter of survival, of life and death, to hang on like mad.

What a come-down! In the beginning Jack had been as
rich and as wide as the world. Rich as the rich world and
wide as the wide world and deep as the deep world — that,
for a little while, had been his thrice blessed state. True, he
had seen off all those heavenly bodies and earthly bodies, but
he had kept track of and kept up with every one of them,
had seen them all safely home. As I say, he had by no means
lost them. He had parked them, and he was their parking
place as well as their proprietor. If ever there was a World
Winner, it had been Jack, all right. But now, without warning,
he'd come so far down in the world that he was easily World
Loser Number One. And, now shrunk to almost nothing
in the cosmic washing machine, his fury knew no bounds.
(Well, wouldn't you be mad if you were a super-tycoon who
suddenly found himself down and out on the bread line?) No
wonder he tried and tried and tried to wreck the machinery.
As Shakespeare said, like an angry ape — or, as we may say,
as an angry ape — he insisted on playing such fantastic tricks
before high heaven as make the angels weep.

Nor did it help that he wasn't quite all ape, that there was
just enough of the old Jack left in him to sense the awful
thing he'd done to himself by defying his father, and trying
to deceive him in this one little matter of his pet monkey. Or
that he knew in his heart of hearts that he only had himself
to blame. No: this knowledge only drove him to play up
more and more.

And what were his monkey tricks, so absurd yet so dangerous and so painful — for others as well as himself — that
they got the choir of heaven howling their heads off?

He brought to a halt what naturally moved, and set in
motion what naturally stood still. He puffed small things up

till they were huge and near to bursting, and squeezed big
things till they all but vanished. Some single things he insisted
on doubling. He twisted and trimmed, sometimes beyond
recognition, practically everything he could lay his monkey
hands on. And whenever he put in a personal appearance he
made sure he was the wrong way up, thus giving notice to
all — in the rudest way he could think of — of his resolve to
stand everything on its head and generally to make mischief
wherever he could.

Of course none of these absurd goings-on was lost on
Father. And of course he wasn't pleased. Here was his dear
and charming boy, thanks to one solitary act of naughti-
ness, become the Bloody Nuisance of the Universe, Nature's
Embarrassment and Pain in the Neck, its Red-nosed and
Unfunny Clown. All the same, Dad didn't care to play the
heavy father and add to his son's self-inflicted punishment.
Still less to force him to come to his senses. No: he decided
to wait and see whether his fast-growing agony would drive
him to relax his grip — his convulsive strangle hold on that
monkey of his — just long enough to let the creature escape
to its proper home out there, where its picture now hung.
Or whether — dreadful thought! — he would play just one
monkey trick too many — the ultimate monkey trick that
would rid the long-suffering world of the trickster forever.

Pause for reflection:

What do you think will happen? Will our villainous hero
kick the habit, get that monkey off his back? Or succumb
to his addiction? Re-infanting or suicide (it has to be one or
the other, there being no third choice) — which will it be?
Do you see Jack becoming himself again and undoing Jacko's
trickery? Relenting, will he set going again all the things he'd

halted, and halt all the things he'd set in motion? Coming to his senses, will he give up inflating small objects and deflating big ones? Will he cease doubling what's single? Will he have the good manners to walk the right way up, the way he was born to walk? Will he? Won't he?

HE WILL! HE DOES!

Yes, he lets go of Jacko and is Jack again. Hurray for the world! Hurray for Jack!

(This is a fairytale, remember. And all good fairy tales have happy endings, regardless.)

Now all the treasures of his infancy, without exception, are dispatched to where they belong out there. Now he's shot of every particle of them, down to the last dust-grain.

Only one snag remains. Not a minor one, I'm afraid. Jack is now absolutely empty, and therefore absolutely poor, far more destitute than ever before. For Jacko-held-onto, though a wretch and a disaster, at least wasn't nothing. There was quite a lot to him. But now there's nothing to Jack, and he doesn't care for it at all.

What had happened to Jack, you'll remember, when he became Jacko, was that he became just Jacko. Shrinking into that one creature had meant shrinking from all the others, losing them to Space. And now that Jacko, too, has taken off and is lost to him, he's back on that vast playroom floor of his, but this time without a single plaything. Not surprisingly, he starts wondering whether being without anything at all isn't just as bad as being stuck with that monkey. Or even worse.

He need not worry. Given time and wakefulness, the problem solves itself most beautifully. No longer that trickster, he stops mucking about with things; and before too long comes, with joy and some surprise, to witness their return to normality. In particular, he allows them to revert to their given dimensions, to re-miniaturize themselves. He sees people, houses, trees, hills, mountains, and stars collapse from the cumbersome giants (each huger and less lovable than the last, and producing still more congestion) that Jacko had turned them into — sees them suddenly collapse into the lovable little darlings that they were originally. For all things, being things, are fairly polite, and can be counted on to make themselves small enough — when not interfered with. Conversely, Jack, being no-thing, is no liar, and can be counted on to make himself big — infinitely big — when not interfered with. Big enough to hold and to fondle countless admirably self-effacing island universes, to say nothing of nearer treasures.

Beautifully small treasures, all of them. Take that oak. Jacko had played the trick of blowing it up to such proportions that — to avoid being overwhelmed by the thing — he was obliged to push it away by a hundred yards. Un-playing that trick, Jack now enjoys an oak he can comfortably handle on the spot, and own, and coincide with, and be. Jacko was far too puny to take on that overgrown tree, Jack is far to large *not* to take on this quite-sufficiently-grown tree. What fun he has now! How delightful life is in this uncrowded Eden, this springtime and morning world! In this park which is Paradise he doesn't see a huddle of big kids over there — probably up to no good and certainly making a horrible noise — but an exquisite corps de ballet whose members are no bigger, and no more rowdy, and no less beautiful than a flurry of brilliant and tiny butterflies. In this heavenly zoo, it's not that, fortunately, Jack's protected from that great big grizzly bear over yonder, but that he's all the way up to and stroking this dear little grizzly-teddy, and he well knows that all little teddies are good and cuddly teddies. Just as all very tiny children are angelic.

Yes, the whole world's beautifully repaired and put together again, as good as new. If not better. And Jack's in Eden, and Dad's darling boy once more. And even Jacko, funny little Jacko getting up to tricks over there (his favourite is pretending to protect himself, behind a sheet of glass, against that wicked Jack) is a good friend and no nuisance at all. For Jack, at last truly free of Jacko, can afford to be Jacko, along with all the others.

And that's the cheerful end to our fairytale. Which we can now rechristen *Jack's Re-infanting and the World's Restructuring*.

* * * * *